UNLOCK
SUCCESS
CODE

The
7-Step
Process to
Succeed in Life and Work

Steve McNicholas

Published by

ISBN: 978-1-9161671-0-0 (print)
ISBN: 978-1-9161671-1-7 (ebook)

Printed in the United States of America

CONTENTS

Acknowledgements

*"There is no better joy than helping others around you
rise up to levels higher than they ever thought they could."*

– Dan Gilbert

In writing this book—from its conception and in helping me frame my thoughts, ideas, and theories that make up the SUCCESS Code® through to the actual writing of the book—I wish to acknowledge and thank many, many people.

To all of those people I worked for, worked with, whom I have learned from, learned with, failed with, and succeeded with, thank you. To those who have inspired and encouraged me, thank you. To those who told me not to waste my time writing one book let alone two and to those who told me to follow my heart and do it, I thank you all.

To those speakers, trainers, authors, mentors and thought-leaders in the field of success and achievement, who kindly spent time with me over the past decade answering my recurring question, "how do you succeed", thank you. Your teaching, coaching and support was always appreciated and I thank each and every one of you.

In no particular order, my sincerest and deepest appreciation goes to the following individuals who, at some point in my life, were kind enough to lead me, work alongside, mentor, inspire, advise and teach me: Martha Bullen, Steve Harrison, Geoffrey Berwind, Tony Robbins, Jim Rohn, Les Brown, Wayne Dyer, Zig Ziglar, Carol Dweck, Brendon Buchard, Paul Morris, Colin Rutter, Mary Whenman, Mark Davison, Bob Munro, Jack Canfield, Steven Covey, Steve Bingham, Craig Donaldson, Ernest Clarke, Michele Dytham-Ward, Esther and Jerry Hicks, Peter Mansfield, Martin Bischoff, Alan Mathewson, Jim Collins, John Tobin, Paul Denton,

Mel Robbins, Barry Connolly, Dean Grazioni, Mark Parsons, Karen Harbishire, Chris Brindley MBE, Graham Lund, Peter Orr, John Berry, John Hesketh, Bill Wilkinson, Rod Bulmer, Gareth Parry-Evans, Brad Fordham, David Ross, Chris Green, Eammon Tierney, Stan Krasnow, Frank McKenna, Andy Fairchild, Mike Davies, Jim Hannon, Mike Gordon, John McAndrew—thank you. To each and every one of you and all those colleagues and clients, past and present, who I have been fortunate enough work with, and learn from, I will always be appreciative of your help and efforts.

To all my close family, my brothers Anthony and Joseph and their families, I love you and thank you all. To the Fish family, thank you for your support, humour, kindness, and love these past two decades.

To my parents, Anne and Joe, your love and support is and always has been amazing. I love you both, and I thank you from the bottom of my heart for everything you did and continue to do for Anthony, Joseph, and me. I hope you are as proud of the men you raised as we are as proud to have you as our parents.

To Caroline, Mollie, and Daniel, you three are my life. You are the reason why I do what I do and chase the dreams that I chase. Your love, encouragement, and support since I first started talking about this book have been incredible. Mollie and Daniel, I hope you will use this book as a guide for your happiness, success, growth, and fulfilment in your own lives, and I wish you every joy and look forward to helping you on that journey.

Finally, to my wife, Caroline, without whom I could not have achieved a fraction of the success in my life so far; I don't have any other words for you than simply to say *thank you, I love you.*

So, Why this Book and Who Is It For?

"One of the greatest things you can do to help others is not just to share and give what you have, but to help them discover what they have within themselves to help themselves."

– Rita Zahara

This book, and the lessons and ideas I promote, is for anyone who knows there is more to life and work than just existing, than just being ordinary. It is for those who know that success in life or achieving in business is something they have to do. This desire burns brightly within you; it probably has for a while, but perhaps until now, it's never been clear just how to turn that desire and need into the success, achievement, fulfilment, and happiness that you know should be yours. Maybe you have tried in various ways, read other books, invested in coaching programmes to try and help you get "there" but without succeeding at this point. This point is now. Over the next hundred and fifty pages or so, I hope to provide you with the steps, the sequence, the "source code" to succeed in all your hopes and aspirations, personally and professionally, but like anything worth doing, you are going to have to own it. If the dreams, goals, and hopes you have are within you, then so is the desire to achieve them. The seven chapters, or Code Blocks as a I call them, that take you through the SUCCESS Code® will test that to the max!

When I consider the reasons that drove me to spend all those long days, weeks, and months in writing this book, I eventually came to realize that I was always going to do this. From leading successful teams throughout my corporate career and through some wonderful achievements on a personal level, for as long as I can remember, I have always had a growing desire to "tell others, help others, create a way for others, and to get on and speak, coach and write about 'it'." I believe we all have "something" in our hearts or in our souls that we truly feel a calling to do. It is often not the job or position we spend most of our time at to earn a living, but it's there. It's the little voice that speaks to you that nobody else can hear. We could call it "intuition" or "gut instinct," but it is the conversation that's always going on in our minds, and my conversation has been going on for decades!

Here are just a handful of the typical conversations I have started with myself over the years! "If you know you want to run your own business helping people, why don't you?" "You know you need to get into a better physical shape so what is stopping you?" "I don't enjoy not winning so why can't my team top the sales league tables?" "If you are going to start a book, why don't you just get on with it?" Do any of these conversations resonate with you? I suspect you have your own conversations going on, and several will start as you get into this book, especially when I call out the moments for honesty, action, or effort. You probably already know what you want and need to do in your life to make you personally happy or more successful professionally because you have probably been telling yourself that for a while now.

I remember listening to one of my most inspiring mentors, the late Wayne Dyer, several years ago when he calmly said to me, "Do not die with your music still in you." That line meant everything to me at that moment in my life, and it still does. It fuels me to push harder when I am mentally or physically tired. It drives me to keep going when I am frustrated or cannot see a path through a problem. I could feel and hear my "music" playing in my soul; it wasn't particularly loud and although I still did not quite understand the "tune" that was playing at that time, I felt certain that I was going to do something about it, eventually. The idea of reaching the end of my life and wondering, "what if…?" scared me witless. Whatever your music is within you—and it could be a whole host of goals, dreams, and aspirations for your life or your career and probably both—then this book is for you. This book, and the talks and coaching I do on the content, that is my "music" and I truly feel alive when it is playing.

If I think over my life journey so far, listing the achievements that you might see on my resume (e.g., jobs, promotions, and the likely trappings of such progress), maybe you would describe my journey thus far in life as a success. These resume documents, a bit like the social media profiles we all have today, almost always mask the true journey that individuals have experienced. I am no different, and the sequence of events that led me to this point in my life, writing this book, and speaking and coaching others on the SUCCESS Code®, has been a journey of progress and failure, of great confidence at times and of considerable doubt at other times, of professional and financial success and apparent security but also several times of worry, concern, and anticipated failure. It is not the type of summary you usually see on a resume or a Facebook page, but it's the journey I have been on and which has helped shape the ideas, concepts, and thinking that this book is based on.

I could summarize the first fifty years of my life so far, culminating with this book, on the arrival in my life of three brown envelopes!

In 1980, growing up in a pretty tough suburb in the city of Liverpool, I was incredibly fortunate at the age of eleven to be offered a place at one of the city's main grammar schools. Grammar schools were considered the elite schools; strong academic track records and success here would likely propel students toward further education, probably university, and wonderful job prospects from there. However, I blew it. I bombed. I was lazy. I always had the attitude of, "I will start studying properly next term," but next term often came and went with the same conversation happening in my mind, "I'll get on with studying soon, I'll do it tomorrow."

It culminated one morning in the summer of 1985. I went to school to pick up my results for the national examinations taken a few months earlier. The school secretary handed me a little brown envelope with my name on it. Inside was a small white sheet, computer printed, with the grades for the ten examinations I had taken, the grades that would be the basis of my future. The letters A, B, and C represented a pass or higher; D and E represented a fail but at least worthy of a grade, albeit a poor one; U represented ungraded; the score was so low that even D or E could not be applied!

My sheet read: E…E…D…U…E…U…E…C…C…U. I was shocked and upset to see those letters in print; my hands were shaking, and then I became angry, very angry. I was angry with the school, the teachers, anyone and everyone, except the one and only person I should have been angry with—me. Those results were the outcomes of my decisions and choices over the previous five years. My choices, my decisions, my results.

On the bus trip home to tell my parents, I think I knew they were expecting bad news despite my false assurances over the years. I was about to let them down badly, the two most important people in my life, and I was looking for any way out of this situation, any way to avoid that moment. I got off the bus and headed to the local café, stopping off at the newspaper shop to purchase a black pen. I had an idea. If I were neat, tidy, and careful, I could easily change each letter U into a D! I could then turn each letter E into a B! I could amend the reporting card from a print with just two examinations passed into six or seven passed and certainly no letter U! My pen hovered over the sheet; my hand was shaking; I was sweating and petrified. I had one chance at this because any slight mistake in making the changes would be obvious. I sat there for over two hours before finally "doing it." The "doing it" was putting the pen away, unused, putting the report card back into its envelope without any changes, and taking it home to Mum and Dad.

I am still haunted by that look of disappointment in their eyes that day. I had been given an amazing opportunity in life, and I had failed. I recall laying on my bed that evening and at sixteen years of age, I decided to take ownership of my life and the outcomes—*for the first time ever*. I finally had a purpose, and it was to make Mum and Dad proud of me again. The goals were clear. Get out and find work. Forget university. Build a career and be the best, most successful person I could be.

Fast-forward twenty years or so. My career had taken me from an office junior as my first-ever job through a number of industries to banking and financial services. I was one of the youngest directors in a major global banking business, leading teams of several hundred people and had all the trappings that such a role provided. Mum and Dad were indeed proud of me and the journey I had taken those past twenty years. But then in 2008, the global financial systems collapsed. Banks literally went bust overnight, and mine was one of them.

I spent a year during that crisis significantly impacting the lives of others. I had to turn up at branches and administration offices and deliver the news of closures, redundancy, and unemployment. It was draining and demanding, but so long as I was doing that task, difficult as it was, it meant I was still employed. Eventually however, it was my turn. A meeting with my boss, and yet again another brown envelope was handed to me that was to bring fear, uncertainty, and anger. I was now a victim of the crisis and with a mortgage, two young children, and a very worried wife at home, the slow and worrying journey began again. This time, it wasn't the school bus that took me home to those I loved. This time, it wasn't the café I sat in and pondered with a black pen, but the fear, worry and anger at the situation was the same.

I sat reading the termination letter over and over again, praying that I had misunderstood the message. I hadn't. I was unemployed in an industry that was imploding globally. My wife Caroline was worried, frightened, and scared. We had two babies and several financial commitments, how would we cope? How do we pay the bills? How do we keep a roof over our heads? Once again, thanks to another brown envelope, I had to stand in front of a loved one and tell her the worst-possible news and see that fear, upset, and worry in her eyes.

I got to work on the computer searching for employment every day. Surely my resume and track record would be in demand. I would be rehired super-quick I told myself—and anyone else who would listen. Sadly, not. A pattern formed. I would spend several hours every day sending off letters, applications, and enquiries about jobs day in, day out. Caroline would come into the room I used at teatime every day and ask hopefully, "Any news?" When I had to report little or no progress, the look of disappointment day after day as she stood in the doorway holding one of our children was heart-breaking; no matter how many times I saw it, it never got easier. The look of hope and excitement in her eyes when I got a positive response was wonderful to see, until as often happened, the enquiry drifted off to yet another decline.

After a number of months repeating the same unsuccessful tactics of applying to the same organisations, extending my range to wider and wider geographical locations, I decided one morning that something had to change, and the only thing that I had the power to change was me. I could not influence the global economy. I could not influence what the government was doing with the banks. I certainly could not change history or undo what had been done. It was a new world, overnight, and I had to change and step out of the career comfort zone or suffer and be resentful, and like many, settle for mediocrity. I chose to change. I took ownership of my situation once again like I had some twenty years earlier, and I decided that I was still the same guy who had succeeded for the previous twenty years with a set of skills and competencies that could be useful in several industries, not just financial services, and when I changed the way I was looking at things, the things I looked at changed!

I stopped clicking the same old boxes on the same old job sites. I stopped speaking to the same recruiters. I joined local networks, full of positive people keen to help me. I called up several new recruiters in other business sectors and I told them about myself. What I could do. What I had done. How I operate. How I could help businesses. Incredibly, the phone began to ring. Interviews started to happen. Optimism and confidence at home picked up, and about a year or so after the last brown envelope, I started a new role in a thriving and growing business services organisation working with several amazing people—several of whom I referenced earlier in acknowledgments—who saw something in me. It's been a gratifying journey of personal growth, professional success, and considerable achievements along the way.

Several years later in early 2018, the business had grown substantially, and we were acquired by a huge global corporate for some $1 billion dollars! However, for good reasons, the new owners no longer needed the managing director—that was me by the way—as well as several other fellow executives. The acquiring organisation had their own successful leadership team who would be running the business from now on. Yet another brown envelope was on its way, and it duly arrived. The previous two brown envelopes brought despair, uncertainty, fear, and worry. It meant delivering awful news to those I loved the most, but this time, things were different.

You will recall at the start of this chapter, I spoke about the dialogue we have in our minds at times and the quiet, personal conversations we have with ourselves, that "music" that plays in our hearts that we must listen to. Well for many, many years, I have always had an interest in understanding and learning more about personal development. How do people improve themselves? How do those considered successful seem to achieve more? How do others appear to have extraordinary success in life or business, and yet the vast majority seem to settle for ordinary? How do people succeed?

That interest, which started in the late 1990s, developed in the new millennium, and gradually in the past decade or so has become something of an obsession! I have spent thousands of pounds and invested tens of thousands of hours over the years in reading, researching, interviewing, observing, and trying to understand the many lessons, theories, ideas, and thinking that many of the leading thought leaders in personal success and achievement from across the globe were sharing. Deep down, I knew this was my purpose, and this "music" playing within me has gotten louder and louder in recent times. It was this last brown envelope that gave me the platform to take the leap from ordinary to EXTRA-ordinary.

Many if not all of us are raised and programmed to be ordinary, to be "average". We are encouraged to study for an education and to try and secure a job, often any job that pays sufficiently. Then we settle down, we check the stereotypical boxes such as relationships and marriage, maybe children, a house and mortgage, pensions, or a combination of all of these. We work and then retire, and then it's done! This is the ordinary path that is often and typically described as the paths of "Mr. and Mrs. Average." I'm not putting down ordinary or average. Ordinary is just not good enough for me, and it should not be for you, either. Ordinary is going through life simply by checking certain stereo-typical boxes, filling out forms, finding a job, paying taxes, being respectable, and trying to remain lawful and *ordinary*. It is about being average at work, in the pack with everyone else, being unfulfilled at work. It's called *ordinary*. It is just about *existing*.

Now, if that is you—and I suspect if you have this book, then it is *not*—this may not be the right choice for you; my path and desire is to experience *the extraordinary*! Yes, of course, you can aim to live an "ordinary" life for the next twenty, thirty, or forty years or more doing largely the same "ordinary" things day in, day out. However, my purpose via the SUCCESS Code® is to help you live ONE amazing, fulfilling, and **extra**ordinary year, and then repeat that year twenty, thirty, forty times over or more!

Extraordinary is something that is completely different. It is about recognizing from within yourself that you have just one chance—one life—to be extraordinary. It is about listening to your heart, to find and live your purpose, to rise up and secure your dream job, to have the most incredible friendships and relationships, to have the energy and finances you need to fulfill your goals and dreams. To be fulfilled, challenged, inspired and to experience success in all aspects of your life and career. All I want to say is this: YOU CAN do so much better than just being average or ordinary. YOU CAN start experiencing and feeling a much higher level of personal and professional fulfillment, of achieving, succeeding in whatever it is that is within you, and then have a sustained level of happiness that follows.

At this point, I will explain how I have come to define *happiness*, and it's a formula I find accurate in pretty much every situation related to happiness that I discuss with clients and colleagues. I appreciate that *happiness* is often described as a feeling, a sense, and sometimes a spiritual experience; however, we definitely feel very different when we describe ourselves as happy. *Happiness* to me is a formula as outlined below:

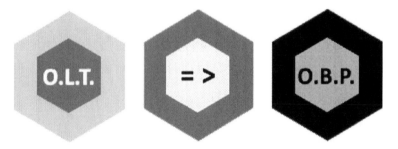

The Happiness Formula: When OLT equals or exceeds OBP

There you go. The happiness formula! What I am trying to say here is that happiness for me is when, "Our lives today" (OLT) is equal to or greater than (= >) "Our blueprint" (OBP). If I asked you to describe what your perfect life would look and feel like if you could have it today, what would you say? After thinking about your health, finances, relationships, career, and material goals, how would you describe it? That description you just came up with is your "blueprint" of the ideal life you want to have. It is your wish list. Now, at certain points in your life when you feel you are at or progressing toward any of these "wishes," you do and will feel happy; that is, you feel energized and excited because this feeling is fulfilling. Even if the ultimate wish is yet to be achieved or materialize, even just the awareness that you are progressing toward it will cause you to feel happiness.

On the other hand, when you are distant or are moving further away from your wishes, your blueprint, you tend to feel unhappy and unfulfilled. The challenge—which I am going to help you with—is to keep moving toward all or as many of these wishes, or your blueprint, much more than you are doing today and leverage the "Code Blocks" to get you there.

In the next section of the book, I will explain more about the SUCCESS Code® and a number of key principles and foundations that you need to understand before applying the teachings in this book. My purpose now in life—the thing I am driven by and feel an amazing, incredible level of fulfilment and happiness in doing—is helping as many people as I possibly can to experience the same feelings I do. You can maybe even call it my mission statement: "To inform, inspire, and help maximize the potential in all people, unlocking the SUCCESS Code® to help develop winners in life and business."

This book and my own personal agenda and passion are wholly based on helping you achieve what you want, be that in a personal sense or also in the business and commercial sense, as the same principles or "Code Blocks" apply in both. In the two decades or so that I have spent learning about personal development, the theories behind achievement, growth, fulfillment, and success, the one shining theme I have understood and will emphasis throughout this book is that if you want to, you can. It is entirely within your ability to do so—it's a gift. This is the first big secret. If you want to, REALLY want to—I mean, REALLY, REALLY want to—you can and you will. I am going to share with you a blueprint, a road map, an operating manual built on the "source codes" on how to succeed, achieve, and win.

Think about it this way: Nowadays, when you buy a new item of technology (a phone, a computer, a TV, a kitchen gadget, etc.), you usually find yourself scanning the instruction guide at least to understand the basics of setting up and switching on the machine and getting the main functions to work. As a human being, you are the most complex, amazing technological machine on this planet. So, when was the last time you flipped through YOUR operating manual to check if everything was working as it should? By keeping a copy of this book, you can be aware of when something isn't working properly in your life, and I sincerely hope that the methodology we'll be discussing will help you reset the machine (you!) to its perfect working order—to the level of personal and professional success and happiness that you deserve and desire—and the time to start this task is *now*, not tomorrow, *now*.

Cornell University in the United States undertook a famous piece of research, *The Legacy Project* (www.legacyproject.com), a few years ago that is still being developed today. It's a wonderful website to visit. The research involved asking thousands of elderly people approaching their end of life a whole set of questions to understand legacy, wisdom, and reflection. A common response from all respondents with little time left was, "I should not have wasted so much time worrying and doubting about things that, in the end, did not matter. I should have chased my dream, followed my passion, listened to my heart, and gone for it then."

Spend a few seconds thinking about what these respondents said. Think about what you're putting off, doubting yourself about, worrying about, excusing away, and blaming others for what you're convincing yourself you can't do, because, frankly, on your deathbed you will realize that those worries, doubts, and fears really did not matter a jot. Sadly, it will be too late then, so let's work together NOW to minimize those regrets and concerns. Let's find success, fulfillment, growth, and achievement NOW!

Throughout our lives, we often settle for far less than what we deserve, and quite sadly, a fraction of what we are capable of. Do this enough and that mind-set and attitude will culminate into habits; put simply, it will define who we are. You may have heard of the expression, "out-of-court settlement." It is used when someone goes to court to fight for something sizeable or to seek a big win of some sort, initially believing in the path he or she is following, but then settles for something far less before the big chance to win arrives. After settling out of court, then comes the dilemma of, "what if?" "What if I had gone to court and really believed in myself, what could I have won?" I believe we all make way too many "in-life settlements." Too often, we settle for far less than what we could achieve—if only we would push ourselves to go for more! This is another reason why I decided to write this book, to tell you how to turn "shoulda, woulda, coulda" into "did it!"

I know you can do it, and I want to help show you how. Here's to your future success, happiness, achievement and fulfillment. That is really why I wrote this book.

Introduction to the SUCCESS Code®

"The big secret in life is there is no secret. There's just you, this moment, and a choice. Whatever is your goal, you can get there if you are willing to work for it."

– Oprah Winfrey

I chose to title this book *Unlocking the SUCCESS Code®* because I really do feel that the content I will take you through is similar to the combination lock of a safe, that when turned in a sequential order opens to reveal jewels, valuable contents, and even treasures! The same principles of unlocking a safe apply to personal development, success, and achievement both in your personal objectives and business life. As adults, we spend the majority of our working hours earning our living in whatever way we have chosen. This effort takes up a significant amount of our time, which is why this book references your business aspirations as often as I do your personal goals and dreams in life.

I think it's critical to highlight at this juncture in this book that by using the words *success, achievement, winning, fulfilment,* and other similar, positive expressions throughout this book, I do not always intend to imply material things that one often assumes to be indicators of success and achievement. Of course, if financial wealth, material possessions, bonus awards, and things such as a bigger home, a faster car, a growing bank balance, and going on incredible vacations are what you aspire to have in order to be successful, then that is absolutely fine. The SUCCESS Code® you are about to follow will enable you to fulfil *all* your dreams.

However, if success and happiness to you mean winning in a different sense—losing weight to be more energetic for your family; learning a new language to increase your promotion chances at work; leaving your job to start a business that you have a real passion for; helping your teams in business perform and exceed targets and objectives—this book and the Code Blocks contained within it will be just as important as anything else that people may use to measure success.

So, what is this SUCCESS Code® and how do we unlock it for the success and achievement that we want for ourselves and others? Well, for over twenty years or more of exploring and developing my interest in this field, I began observing similar patterns or sequences in many of the lessons, theories, interviews and teachings of leading experts and authors in the field of personal development and achievement. Sometimes, these themes would be subtle, whereas other times they would smack me right in the face! Every expert, teacher and thought leader when asked or when teaching their "stuff", would seem to suggest a recurring pattern behind success. Various components may have had different names or badges but in essence, they were effectively the same "thing", well at least to me they were.

Eventually, this sequence, this pattern, or "Code," began taking shape in my mind. It typically was appearing as perhaps eight, maybe nine or ten common themes but I knew the essence, the "source code" of a pattern was there. So, the challenge became this: How could I take these recurring and consistent themes, synthesize them, and then develop a methodology so that such learnings and insights would benefit not just me, but others? With time, the answer became apparent, and the evolution of the SUCCESS Code® began to take shape.

What I have since come to realize and appreciate is that the success and achievements that I have experienced in my own life have come from applying many of the lessons and wisdom of experts, teachers, and thought leaders that I had absorbed over the years from reading their books, materials, and listening to their tapes. I certainly did not connect the dots at the time or understand the SUCCESS Code® that was at play, but now I have realized that I was always applying a number of these principles at different times in my life, often subconsciously, and consequently what I now call "success" started happening.

It happened when my first brown envelope landed. I took ownership of my situation following my poor qualifications, so I needed a plan. I had a compelling purpose to drive me forward, and I set goals and built systems to succeed and progress. I overcame doubts, stepped out of my comfort zone, and did this over and over again. When the next brown envelope arrived, and I was in difficult times during the global financial crisis, a similar sequence occurred, and personal and professional success followed. When I have studied and picked apart the journeys behind many "successful" people, famous and not so famous, I almost always found most if not all of the SUCCESS Code® at play.

To be clear, I certainly do not profess to be a guru on these topics of personal and business growth and development though I know several authors and teachers who are! I would call myself more of a *practitioner*. I have been there, I have worried, and I have stressed and been frightened. I have spent time awake at night thinking is this it, is this as good as life gets? I have made decisions and choices in my professional and personal lives that have worked brilliantly but also had times when everything and anything went wrong! I have fretted about my performance at work, and league or performance tables and those of my teams, and worried about the implications of underperforming. I have had dreams and goals and aspirations about many areas of my life, yet have been, at times, unsure about what to do about them. If that sounds a bit like you, then take comfort, you are not alone! However, take even more comfort and excitement in knowing that we now have the blueprint to change that for the better.

If you consider the amount of material and learning I have acquired, you may say that it has been easy for me (or anyone else who lives this theory) because the knowledge I have gained over the years has helped me. "Knowledge is power" people often say, but well, I fundamentally disagree! Knowledge and then taking action to act upon that knowledge— now that is what I call power! You can read ten or more of the most powerful personal development books ever written, and you could argue you have the knowledge, but unless you apply that knowledge through action or motion or something tangible, what is the point? Where's the power? So what? You read plenty of pages, but without taking action, what is the benefit of seeking such knowledge? The danger with just reading without taking the recommended action is that you collect a lot of books and material that are great for your "*shelf*-esteem" but does little or nothing for your self-esteem.

Do not get me wrong on this point—if you want to understand wealth, you should study wealth. If you want to launch and run a business, you should study successful start-ups. If you want to improve your golf game, you should study golf techniques, and so on. However, in all cases of studying success, you will find the expert or the teacher (or the guru!) clearly stating what you need to DO to achieve wealth, or what you need to DO to launch a business successfully, or the actions you need to DO to hit a golf ball farther. What actions you need to take will be clearly explained. What changes you need to make will be stated. However, this is where success happens—taking the knowledge and acting upon it. Knowledge on its own—what can it possibly do? That's why I wrote this book. I am going to tell you what to DO to succeed in whatever areas you wish to. But then you must actually DO it!

In life, personal achievement, goal attainment, growth, happiness, and success really do come down to a number of logical stages or steps that are applied in a particular order. Each step or block is vital; each leads to the next until success is achieved. I have developed my thinking and approach here and segregated them into seven clear components or stages (or Code Blocks). An overview of the SUCCESS Code® is presented as follows.

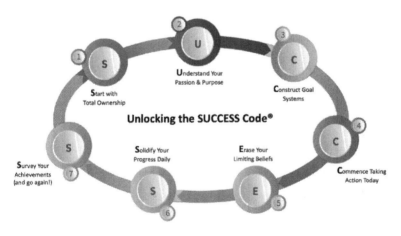

The SUCCESS Code® - A Seven Step Sequence to Succeed

What I wanted to do for this book was to take the research, the core foundations, the great swaths of information in this field, my own experience and thinking and then synthesize all that insight into a *sequence*— a set of simple, logical, practical strategies and actions—that I know will work for anyone who has the desire to achieve and improve. It has taken me a few years to get to this point of refinement, to get to a place where the SUCCESS Code® I will take you through makes sense, and most important, works. Earlier, I had referred to this book as an "operating manual" for personal success, and that is exactly my intention here—to lay out, step by step, how you can make the SUCCESS Code® deliver for you.

In **Code Block 1:** You will understand the significance of taking complete ownership of and accountability for your life, results and situation to this moment; it is 100 percent yours. However, every success and goal you aspire to achieve starts 100 percent with you, and once blame, history, circumstances, and your current situation are dealt with, you can and will begin to unleash your full potential.

Code Block 2: Here we uncover and explore the importance of clarity and purpose behind your goals, dreams, and passions in life. This is the energy and fuel that will propel you during challenging times. Understanding and capturing that purpose in crystal-clear clarity is the platform our goal systems are set upon.

Code Block 3: Now that we have established the foundations, the next step is to set out what our most important goals are and to develop the critical systems to ensure the delivery of these goals. These supporting systems will enable success in several areas of your life, and we will wrap habit and discipline around them to ensure success.

Code Block 4: Here the handbrake is released! This stage is all about action, action, and more action to achieve the goals you have set for yourself. This is when the magic happens, when momentum builds, when success begins to come your way, and when confidence surges. This is when success becomes visible and addictive.

Code Block 5: In this Code Block, we learn how to tackle and erase the "weeds" that plague your mind. Despite your progress, you still need to learn how to do this because your internal *limiting beliefs* are the ones that can derail your progress at any time. Limiting beliefs such as, "it won't work, it is going to fail," will stem from your own mind. You will also be forced to absorb limiting beliefs from a whole variety of external sources, including those who love you.

Code Block 6: Here we build on the previous Code Blocks, solidifying your progress through the powerful techniques of affirmation, visualization, and repetition. The most successful athletes in the world do this before every race or event. The most successful people in business do this every day. It is a fundamental part of your SUCCESS Code®.

Code Block 7: This final block is about reviewing, surveying, and reflecting on the progress you will have made. It is the "self-reflection" checkpoint to ensure all the Code Blocks are followed sequentially and reset where required, and then you go again, and again.

With respect to the number of Code Blocks, you might ask, there are just seven of them? With the amount of information, material, and content I have gathered over the years, I could have easily complicated it by providing eighty-one steps to success. Several books and theories with a purpose similar to this book's do, indeed, take this research and science to such a complicated level that it becomes very difficult to continue progressing following their instructions.

I wanted to create a simple process that you can follow that is not too lengthy and difficult, and after a number of revisions, I realized that seven fits the bill. After all, there are seven primary colours that can create any beautiful image. There are seven musical notes that can form masterpieces that move people to either laughter or tears. The Bible states that God made the earth and all within in seven days. In tarot cards, seven represents drive, success, ambition, and initiative. My son was born on 7/7. My daughter was born on 3/21 (which equals seven). I think the number seven is the right fit.

Each block of the SUCCESS Code® will require you to work through it in detail in the days and weeks ahead, but please do not skip any of them because it will diminish your ability to achieve amazing results. You owe it to yourself to create a life and career of happiness, fulfilment, and satisfaction, a life that you want for yourself, so do not skip any step or try to take a shortcut. I assure you that the time you spend going through all the Code Blocks in order will be worth your effort.

However, you have another option that you can elect to go with. You can go off and spend several years reading, researching, and implementing content from the many hundreds and thousands of books and programs that are available on personal development and achievement. There's plenty of material out there and conducting one search on Amazon or Google will provide you with pages and pages of such learning, thinking, and content. Earlier I listed several experts who can help you get started. It's a very worthwhile exercise as you will attain "success" even if you implement just 10 percent of what you learn from this path. Or, you can simply commit yourself to the process and the SUCCESS Code® that I will share with you. Even if you read and implement one Code Block a week, you'll be well on your way to success in just over a month.

Sadly, on many platforms, there are books, tapes, and programs that suggest that success can be achieved in an instant. The silver bullet is this thing, that thing, or the next thing. I firmly believe that such methods or ideas are misleading and misinforming. Look up any overnight success story and you will find that it took many months, often years, before this so-called overnight success happened. As Michelangelo once said, "If people knew how hard I had to work to gain my mastery, it wouldn't seem that wonderful after all." This is not the book or methodology for you if you want it all by tomorrow. However, it is absolutely the methodology for you if you are prepared to invest time and effort and focus on yourself to attain the success and achievement that you desire.

This book is also *not* a book about the science and psychology behind personal or business development and achievement. I deliberately ensured it *wasn't*. The book is about *action*, of doing, of understanding, and then taking action, of achieving! There are many great books on the science and theory behind succeeding and achieving, and if that is what you're interested in, then please do go and find one. But it's not this one. To be clear, I have tried my best to make every stage of the SUCCESS Code® as easy to understand and implement as possible. Although it is important that you understand the code sequence—the messages, themes, and actions I will ask you to consider—they will not be difficult to understand or implement. You may find yourself going through a Code Block over and over again, but you will only do that because it has resonated with you. It has struck you or stimulated you, which is good!

Let me end this introduction to the SUCCESS Code® by declaring that in my work and research, I often observe three main groups of people in life. The first group constitutes "winners". These people are typically those who always seem to have an excitement and energy and a buzz to their lives, and who continue to be driven to experience more of this success and personal and professional fulfilment. They practice the Code Blocks I will outline, and to them, it's a habit. Then there are the "losers" who simply do not want to improve or grow. To them, others are to blame for everything that goes wrong in their lives. They only focus on what could go wrong and therefore don't even bother to try and succeed.

Finally, the third group consists of people stuck in between the winners and losers, and that's the group I suspect you might be in. You know you want something more and that you are capable of it; you feel it in your heart and soul, and this time, you are prepared to invest all you have to achieve it. You feel that life has more to offer, and you want to go and experience it. You want to enjoy and experience success at work and show others just what you are capable of. You see others experiencing a life of growth, energy, achievement and fulfilment, and you want it, too.

This book will help you achieve it.

Foundational Themes

"Though nobody can go back and make a brand new start,
anyone can start from now and make a brand new ending."

– Carl Bard

Before we get into details about how to unlock the SUCCESS Code®, there are a few foundational themes that I want to address up front that apply in some way or another to every Code Block we discuss. These themes are some of the key foundations that you need to reflect upon and appreciate before we begin this amazing journey. These themes have no order of importance but keeping this in mind, take a few minutes to really think about the following areas and your responses and reactions to each foundational theme. As you reflect on these foundational themes, be aware of the conversation in your head and focus on detecting which voice is loudest—the one shouting, "You cannot do" or the one whispering, "I can do." At this point, it's the whispering that we need to listen to the most, and we need to turn that whisper into a pretty compelling voice.

The "Easy-ness" Conundrum

One of the greatest personal insights that I have developed over the past decade, and which is a core principle in this book, is that attaining an increased level of success, achievement, progress, and growth in any aspect of your life is EASY. The great thing about anything you want to achieve—a milestone, a goal, a plan, a dream, an aspiration, whatever—is that it's often actually very, very easy to do. I mean that, and in almost all cases, I will say it again: It's easy!

In this technological era we live in, you can find the answers with a few keystrokes on Google to every question, problem, or challenge you could ever think of, for example: How do I start a business? How do I learn a new language? How do I improve my personal relationships? How do I lose weight? How do I increase my salary? How can I get promoted at work? Success leaves clues, and there are hundreds of thousands of clues to help you with pretty much every goal or dream, and you do not need to even look that hard. Within seconds, you have all the answers you could ever want. (See, I told you it was easy!)

However, the paradox to a statement like this and a fundamental principle to all success and achievement in life is that whatever we may agree on is "easy to do" is also "very easy not to do," and that is where success and achievement are located, that is, at the very heart of what I will try to convey to you throughout this book. Your approach to this conundrum will become crucially important as you progress through the Code. It is the "easy-ness" conundrum at play.

Those individuals who perform certain fundamental tasks—tasks that, in isolation, are quite easy to do—or engage in disciplined actions (that eventually turn into habits) day in, day out are often the ones deemed to be winning, succeeding, achieving. For some reason, most people who may also intend to undertake such activities just don't. That is the difference between those who succeed and achieve and those who settle for mediocrity, failure, and frustration. A salesperson who makes five more calls every day compared to his or her peers will often sell and earn more and have higher chances of being promoted or sought after by head hunters. A golfer who practices putting for thirty minutes more per week will have a greater chance of successfully putting more golf balls in a round and winning more matches. An individual who goes to the gym for one or two extra sessions compared to others will become stronger, healthier, and fitter quicker. The difference is subtle but HUGE.

Making those extra sales calls is easy. It's not difficult. Putting ten more golf balls is easy. Getting to the gym for an extra session is easy. However, finding an excuse to *not* make an extra sales call or practice more golf shots or go to the gym more often is also just as easy. Sadly the "reasons" or "excuses" we often apply not to undertake these tasks will rarely be of any benefit to you in your pursuit of success. Watching mindless TV.

Trawling social media or whatever else you kid yourself with. Where do you find yourself when you have those internal conversations with your mind—doing the easy stuff as often as you need to, or taking the easy option of *not* doing them?

Nothing I will ask of you throughout the seven steps of the SUCCESS Code® is difficult in itself. In fact, the tasks, reflections, and tools that follow are, in themselves, easy to grasp and apply, but they are also incredibly easy to ignore, excuse away, or simply replace with "better things to do". However, such a choice comes with a price, and hopefully, that's why you purchased this book and finally decided to do the easy stuff.

Successful people strive to do the easy stuff day in, day out more than the rest of us. This is often called *discipline* or *habit,* and I will highlight the power of this in the next section, but for me, what matters most is making a choice at every moment and taking the necessary actions to bring about a positive difference. It's difficult to apply the logic of "easyness" initially, but once you start forming habits to make the right choices every day, you will encounter incredible success.

I am pretty certain that humans are the only species on the planet who have the ability to make a choice about their potential. A tree can only ever be, well, a tree. However, human beings can make the most amazing, transformative, life-enhancing choices every single day. You have the choice to decide how much potential you are going to explore and experience and fulfil. I mean it when I say you can be or do or achieve pretty much anything you want to do. If you deal with the key truths, commit to disciplined action, follow a number of key steps and strategies, it's so very possible, and when you take it down to its simplest level, it is easy.

Discipline and Habit

If there's another common theme that I have identified throughout my learning over the years, it is the *discipline* of *habit,* which is a core

27

foundation of this book. *Discipline* is the bridge between thinking and doing, between inspiration and achievement, between knowing you need to do something and the production of something. By adopting discipline and habits in your daily and weekly strategies, you will experience amazing progress, success, and achievement. Without discipline and the habits that eventually stem from it, you will continue to remain in a state of frustration, or your situation may worsen. Let me try and explain the significance of discipline; it is linked to the earlier point that I discussed about how many things in life are "easy to do or easy not to do." Think about this carefully.

If you know you need to make ten client calls a day to achieve your work goal, but you only make six, you are down by four. If you need to send five prospecting e-mails to achieve the key part of a business goal, but you only send three, you are down by two. If you need to run two kilometres today to keep up with your exercise plan but run only one, you are down by one kilometre. These are just a few examples of how easily you can choose *not* to do something. In isolation, a few days by themselves don't really impact you that much, if at all. However, what we typically say to ourselves is, "Well, that's just today; I'll get back on track tomorrow." Yet, sadly, tomorrow turns into weeks, and weeks into months, and months into years. The cumulative effect of this is horrific on our success, progress and achievement, and once it becomes a habit (good or bad), it is incredibly difficult to break out of. Being aware of what's at stake here is the main antidote. When you understand the significance and critical impact of habit and discipline in personal achievement, success and development, you can begin to leverage the power of this to produce incredible effects.

The best bit about this critical point is that success is based on the complete opposite. By engaging in daily discipline and forming habits to the level you require, you will encounter incredible success. If your goal or plan requires you to make ten calls a day and you make fourteen, you're up by four! If you need to send five e-mails and you send eight, you're up by three! If you need to run two kilometres but you run three, you are up by one! And the list goes on. The important thing here is that by adhering to your goal every day, the positives will run into a hundred more calls, a hundred more sent e-mails, and tens of additional kilometres of exercise. Simple logic states that such discipline will inevitably increase your chances of success and achievement on some level. Moreover, discipline will help you get there faster.

Good habits have an incredible effect on your success; they play the compound game. It's like depositing money in a savings account at a certain rate of interest; you know by leaving the money untouched for well over a time period, the interest rate gets applied every month, and the deposit amount starts increasing. The interest is then paid on the larger, accrued amount, so even more interest is paid. The growth begins to compound, and within a reasonable time frame, the initial deposit compounds to a significant sum. The same applies to your habits. Build and repeat positive habits as part of your journey through the Code, and while you may not see noticeable success immediately, at a critical point when you most need it, the impact will be amazing.

Let's highlight the power of habit in one simple example. Some three years ago, a friend of mine told me, "I really need to lose weight; I'm tired, I'm lethargic, I have no energy for the kids, and the way I'm going, this isn't good for my health. I don't like myself anymore, but it is difficult to do anything about it." As my friend was expressing his concerns, I realized it wasn't an unusual conversation. I believe that the weight issue in this example can be easily replaced with other problems, such as a need to switch from an unfulfilling job to a more satisfying one, a difficult relationship issue, financial worries, career boredom, or personal loneliness. There are hundreds of challenges in your life that you could list or want to improve or change or completely transform. This is just one example.

Going back to the example of my friend, I asked him, "So what's stopping you from losing weight if this what you want? It's stopping you from enjoying time with your kids, so it's clearly important. That is a fairly compelling reason, so why are you overweight? Why are you choosing to not address it?"

And then it started—the blame game! It was everybody else's fault, not his. He had a list of excuses: "No time to go to the gym, and I can't afford one, anyway." "I'm so busy all day; there is no time to exercise, and I'm too tired to exercise when I get home; plus, the kids need me on school homework stuff." "We eat fast foods, and we eat at all times of the day because of our hectic schedules." "When I get home, I just need to chill out and watch TV; it helps me unwind." "I will start to do something about it next month, as we've got Christmas coming up," and so on.

Now, I know I'm being a bit general here, but to lose some weight often takes a two-point goal strategy: 1) follow a better diet, and 2) engage in some form of physical activity. I do not mean to generalize, but this is usually the approach many of us would need to adopt to lose some weight and create more energy and vibrancy. When considering both strategies, I would argue that when looked at simply, following a better diet and physically moving more are "easy" to do.

He is a good friend, and I have coached him in several areas of his professional life using the Code Blocks we are about to learn. However, regarding his weight issue and the impact it had on his life and kids, we got honest about owning up instead of blaming others, and then we got some clarity regarding his purpose. This was NOT about losing weight; this was about being a better dad. We mapped out a few, key disciplined actions and goal systems. (I know this sounds too easy and basic to be effective or true, but it is!)

- We agreed that an important **discipline** to follow would be his finding time to go for a brisk walk *every day*, say half a mile as a start. I didn't care if he had to use his lunchtime instead of sitting and trolling social media in the work cafeteria, and I didn't care if it was raining, snowing, or whether there was a heat wave; he had to go on a brisk walk daily!

- Another important **discipline** to implement was filling his cereal bowl each night before bed and setting his alarm to wake him up ten minutes earlier than usual so he could have a healthy breakfast *every morning* and avoid the Starbucks at the train station. (He told me he went to Starbucks because he did not get up in time, so he was always in a rush with no time to make a healthy breakfast.)

- The third **discipline** we agreed on was replacing the bags of potato chips he ate each day (average of three bags a day) with a piece of fruit. This discipline was linked to the previous one: He would place a piece of fruit by his mobile phone each evening so that he was reminded of taking it with him to work every morning.

- The last **discipline** we agreed on was that instead of watching two to three hours of TV a night, he would look to dedicate an hour to reading about something of interest, one hour spending time with the kids, and then one hour catching up on his TV.

In four weeks, he had lost six pounds! In three months, he was completing three-mile runs several times a week. He was sleeping better, had replaced his potato chip intake with fruit (well, nearly!), and was some twenty pounds lighter. He was really enjoying the hour he spent every night with his kids, and they with him. Yes, of course, he had off days and sometimes went to Starbucks as he had before, but these were exceptions. His new habits, formed from his disciplined actions, were driving him to success, and once he saw progress, the commitment just rocketed.

Previously in my friend's case, it had been just "easy" not to, but in this example the key factor that made his success possible was his daily discipline and his newly formed positive habits. The success was in doing it every day; that's it! To be clear, other key stages of the SUCCESS Code® were also at play here, and you will learn these as we move through the book, but the general principles of this example stand.

Working through each Code Block

As I have mentioned before, this book has been written in a way to take you step by step through the SUCCESS Code®, ideally in the sequence outlined and described in the previous chapter. I won't apologize for the fact that this book, its content, and the flow of each chapter are largely set out in an identical format. Why? Well, it's simply because pages and pages of theory rarely work for many of us. We prefer, in our current social-media-frenzied lifestyles, short, sharp, specific information bursts that are ready to be consumed when we have a few spare minutes to read and absorb them. I have, therefore, rigorously formatted each stage of the Code to help you learn it better, faster, and easier.

The set format and structure of each Code Block allows you to quickly revert to an element or point within a Code Block that you want to revisit. After providing the context to the Code Block, I provide you with five "code-bytes" that hopefully reinforce the message. Some of these code-bytes ask you to complete a task to embed the learning. Some just ask you to reflect and consider what was shared. I then close with three key reflections to summarize the "why" before asking you to complete the "Compelling Action" section. Below is a diagram explaining the structure and approach to each Code Block, and all seven steps of the SUCCESS Code® follow the same approach.

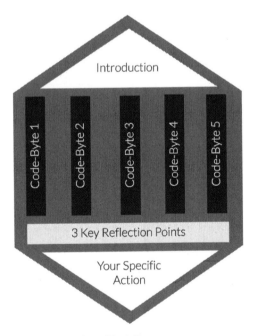

Code Block Structure

The Code-Breaker Toolkit Sheet

This specific subject is crucial, as it will form the foundation of what you are about to start. To help you keep track as you work through the Code, I have developed a tool that I call the *Code-Breaker Toolkit*. This is a vital tool to support your progress and can be downloaded from www.unlockthecode.co.uk. It can be found on the "Resource" page on this website.

You will find that at the end of all Code Blocks, in the "Summary" section, there is a "Compelling Action" that you need to complete. I have put together this tool so you can use it to keep a personal record of your progress. You can print it out at home, fold it into a pocket-sized record, and refer to it daily as you work through the Code Blocks. Please use this tool and the others that will be mentioned later.

Some Questions before You Start

Now, whether or not this is your first attempt at personal or professional growth and development or your seventy-first, the challenges that you encounter in this book will test your intention to take action and to do something to change your life or professional situation. Your mind and thoughts could be telling you to forget it; you can't do this; it is never going to work for you; stay safe and sound in the "comfort zone." It's pretty normal to have such thoughts because they compel you to stay in your comfort(able) zone. However, what you are going to have to do is make a firm decision and ensure that *this time is different*. This time, the desire to change, improve, succeed, and achieve is going to be stronger. Putting yourself in the right frame of mind to apply the lessons and take the necessary actions to unlock the SUCCESS Code® is going to be vital. Here are a few tasks to help you prepare for the stages that follow:

1. **Respect the challenge:** Winston Churchill once said that "success consists of going from failure to failure with no loss of enthusiasm." Irrespective of the areas and aspects of your life that we are going to significantly improve together, you are going

to have to work hard. Understand that when the first challenge arrives, you are going to begin doubting yourself, this book, and your dreams. It is going to be difficult at times, but have no doubt, it is going to be worth it.

2. **Judge the process after, not before:** There are seven stages in unlocking the SUCCESS Code®. Of course, you may skip ahead and try and get into the Code Block that you feel may help you achieve the quickest. I understand and admire that positivity, but I would ask you to apply as much focus, effort, and open-mindedness to all seven stages as best as you can. Follow the sequence. It works best that way.

3. **No short-term fixes:** A little similar to the previous point, we often think there might be a shortcut, a silver bullet, a sneaky, little way to sidestep the process and get to the dream quicker. Maybe there is, and if you find it, I wish you well. However, my experience tells me that this is not the case. The SUCCESS Code® is a sequential process that provides you with an amazing template to succeed. Follow the process, put in the effort required, and appreciate the results of your effort.

4. **Everything we do is to build a habit:** I had discussed the power of habits earlier. Going to the gym for the first time, completing that set of reps, or eating that first salad is not hard. Doing it again and again until it becomes a habit is the hard part. I am going to push you hard, ensuring you commit to pushing through and building those habits. Unfortunately, I won't be able to be with you 24/7, so it is going to be up to you, but please understand why I keep hammering on these points so much.

5. **Use the tools:** There will be several references to toolkits, reference models, or worksheets to help you frame your learning and progress as you apply the Code. Use them! They work! Start right now and download a copy of the Code-Breaker Toolkit from www.unlockthecode.co.uk.

I hope these five specific asks have not put you off from the goal of progressing; these are real and conscious challenges that will present themselves to you quickly if they haven't already. Be mindful of them, acknowledge them, and then push past them.

The Time Is Now

The final foundation to reflect on is *time*. I have worked out that some of the most successful people in the world—the richest, the happiest, or the most fulfilled—get twenty-four hours in their day. Now, we lesser mortals, with gaps in our success or happiness, must clearly get less than twenty-four hours each day. Of course, that's bullshit! We all get twenty-four hours in a day, but the difference lies in what we do with that time. Do we spend enough of it on disciplining ourselves, learning, growing, investing in ourselves, striving toward our goals? Or do we spend it on just moaning, blaming others, watching TV, trawling through pointless social media, regretting, and simply just existing and surviving?

Whatever you want or need to change, it starts with changing yourself. TODAY has to be the day when you finally commit to action, to improvement, to this process. It has to start *now*; no more wasting time and making false promises. I have learned that I can always go out and earn more money, but I can never, ever bring back time once it goes by. Every day matters. When you truly grasp the significance of time and how precious it is, you should not waste another day of your life again.

Few people truly understand how valuable and precious a resource time is. When you realize this and focus and motivate yourself, you can achieve goals in a matter of days that may have taken you months or years previously. Your time is the most valuable thing you "own," and the most precious currency you will ever possess. You can either use and invest it properly or you can waste it in a hundred ways, but unlike money, you can never "earn" it back again.

If you ever want to appreciate time a little more, read books or stories about doctors, nurses, and volunteers who work in a hospice. Take, for example, the *Legacy Project* I had mentioned earlier. Accounts of patients with very little time left are rarely filled with wishes to have watched more TV, to have spent more time in roles and jobs they were unhappy with, to have continued in painful relationships, and so on. When faced with the reality, at the end of their lives, that time is about to run out, many patients talk about wanting to have spent more time on things that mattered, chasing and experiencing their dreams and goals instead of now never having the time to accomplish them.

When you begin to understand and apply the SUCCESS Code®, you will soon realize the importance of your time. We all get twenty-four hours in a day, no more and no less. And we all eventually run out of time as well. I'm sorry for not framing this sentence more positively, but let's be clear: We will all die someday, but hopefully that day is far away. However, when that day does arrive, don't you want to be able to look back and say to yourself, "I gave it my all; I did my best; I regret nothing"? So, why not start this journey today with a clear commitment on how you will invest your time from this point forward?

Decide and commit to yourself that the journey to your success and happiness will start today. Decide and commit that whatever actions and work you need to do to achieve your goals, you will find the time to do it—you will do whatever it takes! Even if you miss an hour of TV each night, so what? You are worth so much more than that. Your time is so very precious; it's about investing it in the things in your life that matter: family, health, personal growth, experiences, memories, a purposeful career, your goals, your wealth, and happiness. Surely, that's got to be worth an hour of missed TV; surely, it's worth it. No more excuses, eh?

I will end this chapter with a poem on time I wrote a while ago. Whatever your age today and however much time we have left as individuals, today should be the day you decide to do it, to confront the truth, accept what's gone is done, realize that blaming is pointless; narrow down what you want to achieve and why, and then comes the best part, the part where you do it.

Time is the gift that can never be cheated,
Once that time's gone, it cannot be repeated.
Your hours each day are a mere 24,
Beggars or Kings get no less or no more.

It's the most precious of things, nobody can steal,
How you spend it each day is your choice, that's the deal.
Get rid of excuses, exchange blame for a goal,
Spend each day with a plan that lights up your soul.

Spend each day with a purpose; have no regrets not to start,
On the things that you cherish, that put joy in your heart.
It's precious and priceless, a possession so rare,
Don't waste it regretting; invest if you dare.

So harbor no anger, frustration or pain,
When you waken tomorrow, invest 24 more again.
Live life with a passion, spend Time on your heart,
Today is a fresh chance to spend Time and start...

...To reflect on these words and just grasp the power,
Of what you can do, in one minute or an hour.
With money and power, you can get into debt,
But with Time, now and past, it's all you may get.

I'm told, "Time is money," of this have no doubt,
That money won't matter when your Time has run out.
Waste no more Time, your mind you must shift,
To make the most of this most precious gift.

So with the time that you have, please do not forget,
Live each day for that moment, have not one regret.
And when the clock stops and the last bell does chime,
How I hope with my heart, you invested your Time.

To Mollie and Daniel, all I want you to do,
Is to spend all your Time being the best one of you.
My greatest wish for you is the gift from "above,"
Of Time to chase dreams with those whom you love.

Have total confidence as you work through the SUCCESS Code®; keep in mind that what the process asks of you is so very achievable. What I will ask of you is honesty and self-reflection, and then, most important, *action*. What I ask of you is a commitment to action and a desire to keep going. Yes, you will have people (often friends and loved ones) telling you not to bother, telling you to stop dreaming, telling you that you cannot. Be strong and push on and strive to achieve all of your dreams, hopes, and goals personally, and if applicable for you, professionally as well.

I wish you all the very best in the days, weeks, and months ahead, and after reading *Unlocking the SUCCESS Code®*, I look forward to hearing of your successes and achievements in whatever it is you want from your life, you work or both.

Code Block 1
Start with Total Ownership

"The moment you accept responsibility for everything in your life is the moment you gain the power to change anything in your life."

– Hal Elrod

A young Cherokee Indian boy was talking to his grandfather about life. The wise old Indian explained to his grandson that the lives we live are simply a result of the battle between the two wolves that live within all of us. One of the wolves, called **Fear,** is characterized by anxiety, concern, hesitation, worry, indecision, and inaction. The other wolf, called **Faith,** is characterized by calmness, conviction, confidence, decisiveness, and action. The grandson pondered for a while and then asked his grandfather, "Which wolf wins?" The old Cherokee Indian replied, "The one you feed the most."

Where you are today in your life or your career, what you've done and achieved or not done nor achieved so far, is pretty much a result of the choices, decisions, and actions you have made or *not* made over your lifetime. That's it. We are all "self-made," but it seems that only the very successful ones carry that label positively, for example: "He's a self-made millionaire"; "she's a self-made entrepreneur."

I think there's a great myth that exists in life today that someone, somewhere, and with some special powers is responsible for making us happy, sorting out the most amazing career choices and paths for us, finding us the perfect partners for life, and generally providing the material things we all want in life. It's just a matter of time, and if we wait long enough, that person will show up, and everything will be fine and dandy. Bullshit! And as my own children grow and begin to experience life, they, too display these signs of entitlement.

I do not mean to imply that any spiritual faith we may have is irrelevant; I am far from that point, actually. My faith as a Christian is important to me and will always be important to me. My point is believing in a different "faith." Many people blindly believe that things for them will change for the better if they just wait long enough. Of course, there are many factors that impact our lives at various stages from childhood to adulthood—our parents, the economic situation, our education, the environment we live in, our physical health and condition—but there is only one person truly responsible for the quality of life you have today, or more likely, aspire to have, and that person is **YOU**. You are 100 percent responsible for everything you experience in your life. I know we're all conditioned to fire off blame—placing it on parents, bosses, spouses, the weather, the government, the bank, the lady you sit next to at work, the economy, the TV, and so on—but it really is me and you, each of us individually, who is responsible.

It's never easy to admit it, but this is a fundamental Code Block in this process that you have to crack and understand: *The life you want to have or maybe the success you aim for in your employment situation is completely dependent on you and you alone.* Although realizing and believing that may be difficult for you to do right now, it is going to be incredibly exciting when you do get to that point of acknowledgment or acceptance. Whatever you want to achieve, in whatever aspects of your life or career, is 100 percent up to you. You own the choices you make each day, and therefore you own the outcomes of these choices. Change the choices, and you will change the outcomes.

It's no longer about searching for or relying on (or blaming) external factors for your current lack of success, achievement, and results you desire in your life. You need to stop looking outside for answers when the most powerful answers are within you. To help you understand this crucial point more clearly, allow me to explain it with a short, fictitious example.

Let's imagine you are in your house; you have your car keys in your hand, but then "BANG"; a power failure and the lights go out, a serious power failure. You can't see a thing, you're in complete darkness, and as you swing and stumble around in the darkness, you drop your car keys. You fumble around for a moment and then realize you are never going to find them in this darkness. You look up and outside through the window, and you notice the streetlights are on. So, in your mind, a lightbulb goes off: "I'm not going to sit around here in the dark, fumbling around for my car keys. I'm going to go out there, under the streetlight, and look for them there!"

You go outside, you are on your knees, searching for the car keys, and your neighbour comes along and asks, "What are you doing, Steve?" You tell him that you dropped your car keys, so he offers to help, and he's on his knees with you searching for them on the ground. Now, there's two of you looking for them. Eventually, your neighbour asks, "Where exactly did you drop them, Steve?" "I dropped them in the house," you tell him. "You mean to tell me we've been on the ground in this street for twenty minutes looking for your car keys, and you tell me you dropped them inside the house; that does not make any sense at all," says the now-angry neighbour.

"Well, it doesn't make any sense to grope around in the dark when there's light out here, either," you retort.

Now, I know this story may seem a little silly, but that is exactly what we do in our personal and professional lives when faced with a problem, difficulty, struggle, or a key choice to make. The answer is almost always located within us; yet, we look for a solution or answer outside of ourselves. Stop looking outside (external factors) for what you want in life; the most important answers and solutions are within you. From today forward, assume 100 percent responsibility for the exciting, positive journey that you are about to commence. Nothing less will do; otherwise, when you come across challenges, and you will, you will revert to blame or guilt or jealousy or unfairness or your past or your parents or your spouse, and so on. That is not the way this first Code Block works.

You have to stop blaming and resenting others in your life, past or present, for what you believe is their fault for where you are today. You also have to let go of those resentments you carry around within you.

41

There can be no place in your future path for any resentment about your past, justified or not. The friend who borrowed some money and never paid you back; the boss who never promoted you when you felt he should have; the client who didn't place the order that was promised; the romantic partner who did not commit to the relationship like you expected—whatever resentments you still hold, you have to let them go at this stage of the SUCCESS Code® because, quite frankly, there is only one person they are harming or holding back, and that's you! You are setting yourself up for amazing success and achievement but accepting total ownership of the journey and letting go of anger and resentments to fully focus on yourself is significant and essential.

There are many critical steps to be followed as we progress through the Code, and rest assured, I'm going to give you several "code-bytes" to help reinforce these points, but everything starts here. Code Block 1 is the primary source code, the most powerful. This one was always going to be the one with the most challenges and the toughest questions and perhaps the most difficult one to grasp quickly and completely. But if you understand the themes and concepts and demands of this Code Block, you are going to do some amazing things in the days, weeks, and years ahead. How do I know this? Because I am aware that when you truly grasp that YOU created your current situation through your choices, decisions, and the paths you chose to walk on, you can also make new choices, different decisions, and create new situations at will.

It is often quoted, and I think it was Albert Einstein who originally said, "The definition of insanity is to keep doing the same old thing but expecting a different outcome." In my mind, that translates into if you just keep on doing, thinking, choosing, and behaving as you have always done, thought, chose, and behaved, you will simply keep on getting what you have always gotten. Nothing will change. However, if you can finally realize that it was YOU who made the choices that got you to where you are today, then it is also YOU who can make the choices to take you where you want to go tomorrow—YOU! For example:

- *You* are the one who ate junk food.
- *You* are the one who bought it.

- *You* are the one who ignored the warning signs.
- *You* are the one who trusted him/her.
- *You* are the one who said yes or no.
- *You* are the one who sits on the couch for hours and watches TV.
- *You* are the one continuing in the job you hate.
- *You* are the one who has ignored your ideas or intuition thus far.
- *You* are the one who abandoned your dream.
- *You* are the one who thinks it is someone else's fault.

In the introduction, I introduced you to the "easy-ness conundrum," and before I take you through the code-bytes to help you really zone in on mastering this Code Block, I want to be honest and transparent here again. This Block is hopefully simple to understand, but it won't be easy to implement, live by, or execute right away. You are going to have to work hard to fight those internal "voices" that will quickly revert to blaming or suggesting external barriers. These voices will immediately suggest it's not your responsibility. They will become louder when challenges arise, but you have to be able to recognize these moments, overcome and deal with them, and begin to build the focus and clarity designed to propel you forward and allow you to live the life you want, expect, and are willing to work for.

Review each of these following five code-bytes and take time to reflect on or do the actions requested. When you get to the "Summary Reflections," I am hopeful that you will have completely accepted the fact that this journey starts 100 percent with you!

Code-byte 1A: Your Push-Ups, Not Mine

Now, this is a relatively short code-byte compared to some of the others we discuss, but this one is perhaps the most critical to your future success. It's no coincidence that this has been numbered 1A.

In many aspects of our lives, we want the quickest solution to our problems. We now have such technology at our disposal at home (the apps on our mobile devices, the internet, computers, etc.) that are designed to get things done faster with as little effort as possible and preferably by others or by other means than ourselves. This, of course, is helpful because it can free up time to spend on other things we may consider priorities. But we have become so dependent on these tools that we are often not prepared to wait or work for anything longer than the bare minimum; we just want "it" and we want it *now*. Success, achievement, and goal attainment in life and business will always take time and effort, but it is time and effort that is so worthwhile when the results begin to show.

Let's use a potential goal of getting fitter, healthier and stronger at the gym as an analogy to help you better understand this concept. You can hire the most qualified and expensive personal trainer in the market, with a great website, impressive credentials and wonderful promises of his or her capabilities. However, after filling out the forms and maybe measuring some vital body signs, it's eventually YOU who has to do the work. YOU have to get on and use the equipment. YOU have to sweat and ache for the results you desire. YOU have to do the push-ups; nobody else can do them for you. If you pay someone to do push-ups for you, you will never, ever see the physical, health and mental benefits of the exercise for yourself, and you will be financially poorer with nothing to show for it!

From now on, you are going to have to own the fact that you are the outcomes of your choices. You cannot continue to let life happen to you; you have to *make* it happen for you! This book will tell you how to achieve, succeed and create the life, business and career you want but these are your push-ups, not mine. I cannot do this for you, nobody can; this is going to be yours to own. In this Code Block, you are the only person who can accept ownership and do this for yourself. Doing the first push-up is usually easy, as we are all capable of it. However, the second one is a bit harder, and it keeps getting harder the further you progress; but the more you work out, the stronger you get and the less you find yourself seeking excuses. You will be responsible, you will be owning the "push-ups," and from then on, you will build the energy, the confidence, and the strength to take on anything. Taking responsibility for your thoughts, actions, and life can feel challenging. It requires a willingness to learn from your mistakes, to overcome the doubts and fears that will surface, and to stop blaming others for your circumstances. But taking ownership of your life also builds character, grit, and self-respect, and in this case, we build muscle.

Don't look for the silver bullet in applying the SUCCESS Code®; it's you, only you, who can do this; so take a deep breath, metaphorically get down on the floor, put your hands on the floor, push up and go! This is your life we are going to change. Remember: These are your push-ups, not mine.

Code-byte 1B: The YOYO Formula (You Own Your Outcomes!)
I quoted Einstein earlier, and of course his theory of relativity is one of the most famous formulas in the world. Most of us know $E = mc^2$, but unless we are planning to win a Nobel Prize sometime soon, I am not sure how relevant this formula is in our lives. I am not sure the vast majority of people can explain it or even understand how it works. Yet, we know it. We quote it. It's in our heads, as we have heard it being quoted so frequently at school. There are many such significant formulas, especially in the worlds of physics, mathematics, and science.

However, there are a number of formulas in life and business that I believe are considerably more relevant and practical for us to master than the one for relativity. When it comes to understanding and mastering this first Code Block, I want you to understand and grasp the following formula:

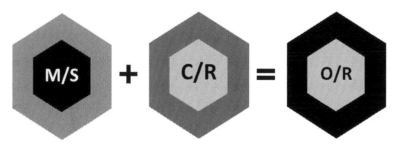

The YOYO Formula: You own the outcomes in your life

*The **Moment/Situation** plus your **Choice/Response** at that moment or in that situation, equals the **Outcome/Result** you experience.*

The basic rule of the formula is that every outcome or result that you experience in any aspect of your life, is a direct result of the choice or response that you made in specific moments or situations. Think of any aspect of your life where you feel unhappy or dissatisfied, and then honestly think of the decisions or choices you made at various moments that led to this position, and then you will understand why you got the result or outcome you have today. When I am unhappy with my weight and my general health and wellbeing, I can quickly recall countless moments or situations when I had the choice to do something about it. I made decisions, mainly poor ones, that led to an outcome of declining health and wellbeing. If I had made different choices or responses, I would have had a different result.

If you are unhappy or unfulfilled or disappointed with the outcome or results you are having in life or business, you effectively have two levers to affect this "formula."

The first lever is to blame the moment or situation you found yourself in. In other words, you can blame the weather, economy, government, client, or the system; you can blame your boss, parents or spouse, equipment, the price of your product, the scale of the goal you set for yourself, and so on. You can even apply more emotive factors such as racism, gender bias, or educational circumstances. Now, there is no doubt that these factors and situations actually exist, but if they were THE critical factor in this formula, nobody would ever succeed at anything in life. Would Obama have become the first black US president? Would Steve Jobs have founded Apple? Would Roger Bannister have run a mile in under four minutes? In more practical situations, would *Fred* have always been the top salesperson in your organisation? Would any client ever buy any product or service? Would anyone of average height, weight, or size have run a marathon?

For every reason or factor that you believe prevents you from succeeding, trust me when I say that there are thousands, maybe millions, of people who have faced the same situations or moments, often much more challenging than yours, and still succeeded.

I play golf occasionally and usually at moments in the game when it really matters, I always play badly. Typically, I blame my clubs and equipment for my poor shots and poor game. As a particularly tall guy, I'm well over 6 feet tall, I even blame my height! However, the opponent who beat me in the last game I played had the very same golf clubs as I did! So is it really those external factors—my golf clubs—that are to be blamed for the result I ended up with? Or, is it me and my choices or responses to the situation? Let's reflect on this. I have never chosen to try and improve my technique with golf lessons despite losing all the time. I never responded to a loss by arriving super-early for the next match so that I can practice my game beforehand. I always seem to have a negative attitude before the game, another choice I make, expecting to lose before the first shot is hit. Yet, if so many people can succeed and achieve in life and business despite similar external and so-called limiting factors, then so can you.

So let's look at the second part of this formula, the other lever we can pull to change the outcome or result to something more positive. This lever is the choice or response we make in such moments. You can change your attitude, the way you plan your day, the way you react, the negative images in your mind. You can change any behaviour or thought that you know is negatively impacting your outcomes. You have that choice. You have the power. It is 100 percent in your control to do so. You can choose to change your mind-set, attitude, or opinion you have in any situation or moment, and the outcomes or results that follow will be considerably different!

Right now, you may be stuck with the conditioned "choices" that you made during these moments and situations in your life or career to date, but to succeed, achieve and grow, you are going to have to try and take back control here to effect a different result or outcome that you desire. It can be a scary but pivotal moment when you think hard about this formula and ultimately discover that your default position is to generate a negative response or restricting choice in those moments or situations when performance, happiness or success is at play. If you keep your mouth shut when you know you should speak up, if you know you need to share your feelings with a partner but avoid the conversation, or if you fail to accept it's you that owns the outcomes or results and you revert to blame, then you are never going to experience the progress, achievement, and success in life or work that I know you yearn for. You are never going to stride toward your goals until you accept this formula, embrace it for the positive tool that it is and push through and change the choices and responses you make.

Code-byte 1C: Awareness of the Three Controllers

In almost all situations in life, when we face a challenge, situation, or even an opportunity, in our minds, at any one point, we have control over three things: first, our thoughts— what we *think* right at that moment; second, our imagery—what we *see* at that moment; and third, the *choices* or *actions* we make as a result of the first and second controllers. Pretty much every other factor in any given situation is beyond your control.

Let's say you planned to go for a run as part of your exercise goals. You wake up to a wet and cold morning. Then, within seconds of waking up, you start to form images of how cold and horrible it is and how much nicer and warmer your bed is. You *think* it's too cold and wet. You *see* the hassles of getting up, getting dressed, and the rain lashing at you, drenching your clothes; you *see* the big hill you don't enjoy. You finally *decide* it's not happening and make the *choice* to stay in bed. But when you look at the X on your exercise plan later that morning, you regret not getting up and going.

Another example: You are in a meeting at work with lots of colleagues, and you get a great idea for something you are all working on. You think you should say something and share your idea, but then you start imagining what your bosses will say and think. You *think* it will be considered a silly idea and you *see* yourself ridiculed by peers, so you *decide* to keep quiet; you say nothing and then you regret it all day.

Another situation: You have been frustrated with your romantic partner about something that has been nagging at you for weeks, and you know you need to discuss it with your him or her and work it through but you *think* that today is not the time to raise it. You *see* the conversation going badly, your partner exploding with anger and making the situation worse, so you *decide* and make a *choice* to say nothing, smile as if everything were okay when it is clearly not. You go to bed again that night and lay there regretting not saying anything and find it difficult to drift off to sleep.

In all three scenarios, you were in complete control of the key factors (three controllers). The thoughts you had were yours. The pictures you imagined were yours. The choice of action you made was yours. And all three led to consequences you now have to deal with. All three consequences are 100 percent your problems; if these situations are one-offs, then this is not a big problem, but if you tend to let these three controllers operate negatively most or all the time, you will always have an issue with your personal development and desire to achieve.

Consider the opposites and what would have happened. You didn't see the negative, you saw the chance to build on your progress and anticipate the pride you will feel crossing off the run on your exercise plan. You got up, you got dressed, and you went for your run—yes, in wet weather, but the satisfaction of completing it would have been worth it. There would be a check on your exercise plan chart. You would glow while having your shower, thinking, "I did it," and you would feel energetic all day after exercising. All this is 100 percent possible and within your control.

Now, imagine the second scenario. You cleared your throat, you spoke up, and you shared your idea at the meeting with your colleagues. The idea is debated over, and people generally think it is worth pursuing. You feel a buzz, thinking you were able to help, and your boss appreciated you for that. You build a little bit more confidence to do this again the next time you're faced with a similar situation, and your day just seems to be better as a result. Again, this is all 100 percent possible and within your control.

Now, the last scenario. You turn the TV off and express your concerns to your partner. Your partner is glad you did so because he or she could tell you were not happy of late. You both agree it's something you should work on together; you make some plans to do so to prevent it from happening again. You have great sex and you sleep soundly without these worries on your mind. This too is all 100 percent possible and within your control.

We discuss some great techniques and tools to help you break through such situations when we get to Code Block 5, (Erase Your Limiting Beliefs), but very often just being aware of the "three controllers" is enough to make you change. When you know and feel the moment, the situation, and the opportunity presenting itself, try to push through, cut out the negative imagery, or prevent yourself from imagining the negative consequences, and take the right action! I am not saying it is easy; it is not. But the effort is worth it to give yourself a taste of how powerfully fulfilling your life can become when you begin to control the three controllers.

Code-byte 1D: The Accountability Seesaw

I hope you are beginning to understand the significance of your "owning" your future. You cannot go back and change a single aspect of your past or change or influence yesterday; it is gone, done, happened. However, you do have complete control and ownership of today. Tomorrow has not even arrived yet, and when it does arrive, it will be called "today," so today is what you can control.

Take a moment to reflect here; think about where you typically "sit" on the seesaw in the figure below when faced with key moments, important decisions, and personal choices that impact your life and happiness.

Where do YOU typically 'sit' when YOU are presented with Moments and Situations that challenge you - but could change YOUR Results/Outcomes?									
Just Gets On With it and does it!	Finds Ways to get it done	Owns the Challenge	Appreciates Reality Here	Seeks Reality	Avoids Reality	Fights Reality	Blames, Blames, Blames!	Personal Excuses	Wait and Hope!
5	4	3	2	1	-1	-2	-3	-4	-5
"OK let's do this!!"	"What can i do here?"	"If this is to be, It's down to me!"	"So this is the way it is then"	"So what's happening?"	"I'll say nothing"	"That's not how I see it"	"It is all their fault"	"It's not MY job!"	"If it's meant to happen it will"

Enabler

Life Happens!

Victim

The Accountability Seesaw: Where do you typically 'sit' when life happens?

Clearly, progressing and "sitting" on the lighter side of the seesaw is the place to be, and the closer you are toward the "Enabler," the better. You have to be honest with yourself when you look at this model and the language used in the example. There is no point in kidding yourself that you are a 4 or 5 under "Enabler" when you know in your heart that you are typically in the dark areas when dealing with those choices that impact your outcomes. The point here is that you need to realize the impact of where you are sitting. If you are "sitting" too much to the right (the darker side), you are typically going to find yourself as the victim. Fault, blame, rationale, excuses, the usual array of victim features will be the weight that tips the seesaw toward "Victim." However, as you become more and more aware of this significant Code Block and its impact, you must work hard to shuffle along the seesaw to the lighter side. The outcomes here are clearly enabling ones. You will have to own them. You will have to take ownership of your actions. You are going to enable your success. Remember, such moments and situations can change YOUR life (its outcomes), so until you realize and appreciate the power of owning the "Enabler" seat and moving away from "Victim," is anything ever going to get better?

Code-byte 1E: Just Two Types of Problems

When I am coaching clients and we are at the beginning of this process—in the very same Code Block as you are now—I often have an almost identical conversation when we begin exploring why we are where we are today. I almost always hear some raw emotions playing out under the theme of excuse, blame, or lack of ownership. There is always some reference to external factors (work, family, employer, partner, spouse, time), and this happens even before we get to discussing all the other problems that the individual faces each day of his or her life, so the lists here can be short or long, but they are most often long.

You will understand a little better now even at this early stage of the book that until you get your head around the code-byte 1B "YOYO" (You Own Your Outcomes), it's going to be really tough progressing to the other six Code Blocks as your mind will not be set up for success, achievement, and taking ownership of your life, job or results. Where you sit on the accountability seesaw, for example, is key.

Now, let's go back to the lists of problems. If I look at the notes from these discussions with my clients, many of whom have gone on to achieve amazing personal successes and goals by the way, there's often a common theme I notice across the pages of my notebook detailing these conversations. Here's a few that typically crop up at the beginning of the journey through the Code.

- **Time**—My clients usually complain of not getting enough of it.

- **Age**—My clients think they're too old for any of this stuff.

- **Money**—They think they don't have enough yet.

- **Family**—They feel everyone needs them, leaving them drained.

- **Physical Shortcoming**—They are either too small, too tall, too fat, or too skinny.

- **Their Boss**—They think their bosses don't like them, rate them, even know them.

- **Their Partners**—They feel their partners don't support them.

Other issues include, "I can't cope with the risk of doing this and failing"; "It is too scary"; "I hate change"; "I will be ridiculed if I fail"; "Success is for others, not me"; "Why bother, anyway?" The lists can often go on for several pages.

However, what I have come to discover myself is that there are actually only ever two types of problems we face in our lives: **permanent** and **temporary**. That's it, really; every problem we have ever had or ever will have in life, can fit under one of these headings, and I will often ask my clients to categorize their own perceived problems under these two broad types.

Permanent problems are those issues that we just cannot change: our age, the time we have each day, how tall or short we are, our skin colour and nationality, our past and what we did or did not do, a disability of some sort, how other people think and behave and the choices they make. There are more, but the point I want to emphasize is that these problems are never going to change, and you have zero control and influence over them. You can't change them or make them different. It is what it is, and spending time and energy and emotion worrying and being drained by such problems is rarely productive. You cannot change what you did two years ago. You can learn lessons, of course, but you cannot change it. You cannot become a foot taller because you would like to be. You cannot make other people behave in a different way just because you want them to. Please stop wasting your precious time and energies on these permanent problems. They are holding you back from addressing the problems you can fix, and no matter how much you think you can and want to, it's not going to happen.

So, we can now focus on the temporary problems. These are NOT fixed. These you CAN change. These you do have the power to change quickly—your body, your relationships, your boss, how you spend your time. These are the types of problems that warrant your time, focus, and energy because you have power here to "control the controllable."

A very powerful task to perform to help you here is to take some time and just list on a piece of paper or in your journal what your temporary problems are. List them all. Then, next to each problem, ask yourself, "What can I do to fix my problem?" At this stage, you should not be looking for perfect solutions but rather just listing as many ideas or thoughts on what you could do with each problem. Even if you are not sure if you're capable of executing them, don't let your brain interrupt you with all the reasons why not; list them down and keep writing.

For example, you declare that you are unhappy in your role and that you really cannot see a way of progressing if you continued to work there. This is a temporary problem. It can be changed. You are disengaged with work, you are not enjoying it and it's impacting your energy levels and general happiness and how you feel about yourself. You want to change job and will no doubt be setting a goal to do so. So, start to brainstorm and list down "what I can do to fix this problem." Look into what I want to do. Go on the job websites to explore. Set up a meeting with a career adviser. Talk to a mentor about what I need to do. Speak to people in my network about opportunities and introductions. Research several companies I would like to work for and send my resume for consideration. Look into some additional education to broaden my experiences and competencies. Just keep writing and brainstorming. I suspect you can make a long list, but you are simply creating options to address a temporary problem—a problem you can do something about. It's not permanent; it's temporary, and while you may not be able to take all the actions you are listing, your brain is already switched into positive mode thinking of ways to address this temporary problem for you. Keep listing and keep thinking, "what can I do to...." Don't start being distracted or worried about the resources you may or may not have; keep working on the "resourcefulness" part—that's how you keep the ideas flowing and the list longer.

The longer the list of what you can do to remove this temporary problem, the easier it is for you to find solutions. When you have exhausted your list, the task now is to look at which of your ideas or suggestions you can implement or do NOW. Pick three, maybe four, that you can start to implement today, and just start. Take each day as a fresh start. Focus on doing todays tasks and give no thought to tomorrow or yesterday. Focus in on today. We will develop "goal systems" in much more detail in a later Code Block but don't wait until then to begin tackling your temporary problems! Even the smallest steps of action today will make a difference, mentally, physically or emotionally.

You have two sets of problems remember, but there's only one set you can do something about, and the great news is that the set of problems you can fix is temporary. The problems on the list can be tackled, addressed or erased, so you need to "own" this list and spend time focusing on the problems you can do something about, and spend zero time focused and distracted on those problems that you cannot influence, control or change.

Summary Reflection 1

We often hear medical professionals say, "You are what you eat." Whatever you fuel yourself with manifests itself through your body shape, fat levels, blood pressure, risk of heart attacks and diabetes, and so on. I think that the same is true for those who want to achieve in life, to win, to succeed in business, and be fulfilled and happy in the general sense. We have to fuel ourselves with positive attitudes, habits, mindsets, and strategies that will support that desired outcome. How can we expect a positive outcome if all we "fuel" ourselves with is thoughts of blame, anger, regret, bitterness, and negativity? This Code Block started off with the fable of the two wolves; which one will you choose to feed while moving forward today?

Summary Reflection 2

Whatever you want from your life is entirely within your capability, control, and influence. However, you have got to do this; nobody else is going to do it for you. I had earlier made a point about doing your own push-ups to build your muscles. This is equally true for life in general, especially when it's about your dreams, goals, and aspirations. Those dreams and goals are yours, nobody else's. So, you have to own them 100 percent; you have to accept that if they are going to be fulfilled, it's you who is going to do so.

A very famous movie was released in 1982 starring Tom Cruise and Jack Nicolson. This movie was set in a military courtroom and was called *A Few Good Men*. In the most pivotal moment of the movie, Jack Nicolson as a senior US military leader passionately bawls out Tom Cruise's character, stating, "You want the truth, but you can't handle the truth!" The first step to achieving any kind of personal or business success is being unequivocally honest with yourself and the choices or responses you took to get you to this point. Make no mistake about it, everything begins with the truth, and being honest with yourself requires one very critical thing that is very often overlooked—taking ownership of every choice, decision, and action you have taken, and more importantly, are going to take today and in the future. One of the reasons that Thomas Jefferson famously said, "Honesty is the first chapter in the book of wisdom," is that being honest to yourself and taking ownership and personal responsibility for your actions are sound wisdom behind any plan, process, or strategy to improve personal happiness, attain fulfilment, and reach your goals.

Over time, failing to accept responsibility and ownership for your decisions and choices has severe consequences. First and foremost, it has a devastating effect on your mind-set and heart. When you know you have failed to take responsibility for something that you should have, it'll begin to bother you, to eat at you little by little. Pretty soon, you'll feel very small inside. Sometimes, especially when we're young, we don't always see the long-term effects of our choices, decisions, and attitudes. But, make no mistake, accepting responsibility for those things now and moving forward is a fundamental part of the success I know you are going to achieve as a result. Look in the mirror and feel that the person looking back is going to completely own the rest of his or her life and the success, happiness, and achievements that will inevitably follow.

Summary Reflection 3

Be aware of the formula **M/S + C/R = O/R** (Moment/Situation and the Choices/Responses you make which drive the Outcome/Result you get) and look how it applies itself in your life and career dozens of times a day. It will happen in about thirty seconds. When you get to the final part of this Code Block, I will set you a specific action to complete your *Code-Breaker Toolkit*. You will be presented with a choice then: Are you going to bother to do it, or not? The choice you make will determine an outcome or result. Is it going to be the outcome and result you want? Will you will move forward or not.

*Compelling Action 1*_____

Update your *Code-Breaker Toolkit* sheet under Code Block 1. Enter THREE positive, personal and powerful statements to confirm that you will take complete ownership of your life, results and goals from NOW.

Example: *I know that I want to achieve X in my life so from today, I will assume complete ownership of every decision and action to get me to X and I am totally determined to do this for me and my family!*

_____

Code Block 2
Understand Your Passion and Purpose

"There are two great days in a person's life. The day we are born and the day we discover why."

– William Barclay

If Code Block 1 has resonated with you, and you have reflected and committed to the statements in your *Code-Breaker Toolkit*, then well done. It's only a start but accepting ownership of your future success and achievements is a significant step! You are off on the most amazing journey, so let's move on with Code Block 2, "Understand Your Passion and Purpose."

Now, many books, courses, and programs on self-improvement, business management, or personal growth (many of which I have read, tried, or considered) delve almost immediately into the power of goal setting. Search Amazon and other sites for books purely on goal setting, and you will find several thousand to select from. Do not get me wrong; goal setting is a powerful mechanism to support goal attainment, and it plays a significant role in the SUCCESS Code®, and we discuss it in the next Code Block. However, I am going to be very clear here: There is a crucial stage, or Code Block, to cover before we move on to goal systems, and that is clarifying your purpose or passion. In other words, we are going to explore and seek real clarity on your "whys," your "drivers," your "motives," your "reasons." We drill down to what you feel your true purpose in life is and what will make you the most fulfilled and happiest when you are progressing toward it.

Before we begin that process, let me clarify why this Code Block occurs before the one dedicated to goal setting and systems. One of my goals that I have been working on for a couple of years now is writing this book, *Unlocking the SUCCESS Code®*. It is in your hands now, or on your device, or whatever, but the goal has been achieved, and I am proud and happy with the outcome of this goal. However, this is only one of my several short, mid- and long-term goals, and all of them have been created to help me progress toward a "purpose" and also fuel a "passion".

While the **goal** was to write this book, the **purpose** was so much more emotional, so much more compelling, and so very personal to me. I may have mentioned it earlier in this book, but my purpose for the past few years has been "to inform, inspire, and educate people with a strategy or process to help develop winners in life and business." It is my passion, my rocket fuel, as I see it, to use my knowledge, experience, ideas, and insights to help people unlock their individual codes to success. I want to leave a legacy for my children to use and apply. I may help only five people, maybe a thousand people, hopefully tens of thousands of people, but it is a purpose that drives me and motivates me every waking day because it is so much more than just me. It is something deep within my very being, my spirit, my soul, whatever and wherever it is that sits within me; it is a powerful force that drives me forward time and time again.

When the moments arise in progressing my goals, when the distractions present themselves, when the chance to stop writing and leave this book to one side comes up—and there were many such moments over the period it took to write this book—I knew I could not. Once I reminded myself of my purpose, it was just too strong to allow me to stop or be distracted for too long. I have people I want to help and they need my help so I have to keep pushing on. That's what this Code Block is going to get you to consider, to address, to try and define, because when you have this—your purpose and passion—and it's clear and understood by you, the attainment of your goals, the next Code Block, will become so much easier and likely!

In business, aiming for targets, quotas, or objectives is pretty standard. Most businesses, and individuals within, fail or succeed on the level of progress they make in hitting these metrics. However, in most business situations that I have worked in including my own business, the level of achievement is pretty much correlated to the level of effort, engagement, and focus of the teams within. For example, when a sales team is operating and aligned with a powerful collective purpose and every individual "buys in" and owns it for themselves as well, there really is not much that can stop their success! When everyone on the team understands and buys into the "why" both for themselves and for the entire team, incredible success is pretty much guaranteed. However, when there is a disconnect in purpose, then there is a lack of passion and progress, and performance is compromised. It's that important. No matter what the goals are, unless there is purpose and passion clarified and understood, there is a real risk those goals won't be met.

I firmly believe that within each and every one of us is a *purpose*, a reason we are here, and, ultimately, a direction we "feel" we need to head toward. Sadly, the world we live in is designed to scare us from pursuing such a purpose. We hear the "music" often in our hearts; it's those moments when you say to yourself, "I would really love to…." The sentence is often finished with a dream, desire, wish, or purpose so inspiring to you, so uplifting, that it makes you feel alive and excited about what it would feel like to fulfil it. Then the world and reality take over, and you're flooded with the reasons you can't, or shouldn't, or couldn't, and the "music" stops. But it never goes away. It is always playing quietly in your heart and soul, and it's waiting for you to start listening again. That "music" is your purpose; it's what your heart and soul are telling you to explore, to examine, and to go and do because that is what life achievement and success are ultimately about. I want you to listen to your "music" and explore what it is saying and trying to tell you. As I have mentioned earlier, the brilliant Wayne Dyer once phrased it most wonderfully, "Don't die with your music still in you."

I have coached clients who came to me frustrated with the lack of progress toward their goals such as losing weight or getting promoted at work or launching a business. This frustration of not achieving or progressing often arises because of one common failure: **We don't get what we want because we don't know what we want!** I may generalize with such examples, but at least having such goals is considerably more powerful than not having any. However, when digging for clarity and purpose behind these goals, we eventually get to the fuel, the juice, the energy, the "music" that was going to power these goals toward a successful conclusion. It is this clarity that leads to the power to act and do. Without this clarity, we often run around in circles, getting nowhere, becoming frustrated, and perhaps understandably, despite our best intentions time and time again, giving up. That's why understanding your passion and purpose comes next in the SUCCESS Code®.

Sarah's goal was to lose some weight. According to Sarah, she wanted to lose some weight to improve her overall health and boost her confidence for a forthcoming holiday. However, she soon started feeling frustrated as the goal was proving to be too difficult, and her trips to the gym were becoming less and less frequent. After some discussion and using some of the tools and techniques that follow, it transpired that Sarah really wanted to lose weight to try and prevent the onset of diabetes, which she had been warned about during a health check.

This was made even more personal when she explained that she wanted to improve her weight and overall life expectancy because she wanted to see her daughter get married and hopefully live to see her first grandchild. Now, that is purpose! That is going to be the fuel, the energy, and the juice that drives you when a goal becomes tough. When the goal plan says go run in the park today, and you don't fancy it—it's cold, your legs feel sore—I know you'll have a much greater chance of getting out there when you remind yourself of the purpose—living long enough to meet your grandchildren.

You see, there is a price to pay for our dreams and goals. I don't necessarily mean a financial price, but success takes time, effort, and guts, and when it's a really big dream or goal, it can take blood, sweat, and tears. When you have clarity and purpose behind your goals, however, then there is no price you won't be willing to pay to achieve them. You will be pulled toward success rather than having to push yourself; that is why clarity of purpose, unleashing your passion, is so crucial.

So, that's what I want you to consider as you reflect on the code-bytes in Code Block 2. I hope one or more will resonate with you to help you understand your purpose, your passion, in as much clarity as you can. As in the previous Code Block and in the ones that follow, take time to reflect, make notes in the book or in your journal, be honest with yourself. I sincerely hope when you get to the end of Code Block 2, you will have unlocked the fuel, energy, and power of purpose that is going to propel you toward amazing success in whatever aspects of your life you desire.

What follows are five code-bytes to consider regarding your understanding or approach to this next part of the SUCCESS Code®. Consider and reflect upon each one in turn, taking the required action or actions that you feel are most appropriate to your situation or challenge.

Code-byte 2A: Understand Your Purpose

When asked, so many people think that their jobs or careers are their purpose and they get lost in the fact that their jobs today, yesterday, or tomorrow are simply achievements. Warmest congratulations if you have the job of your dreams today, but for most people, your true purpose is often something separate from your present position or career. It is separate from how much money you earn a year or how many people work for you or the objectives on your job description. *Your purpose is your core.*

Other people think purpose is some higher calling, some divine task or mission that can only be revealed by some spiritual force or by meditating and chanting naked outdoors every other weekend! While your purpose may well be a form of some higher and meaningful plan to leverage your talents for the greater good of mankind—and I'm going to steer well clear of challenging anyone's religious beliefs here—few people today find their purpose by going on a pilgrimage.

This is a fact; it is reality because we know it is true. Life, my life, your life on this planet is not forever. We have a certain amount of time here, and the vast majority of us have no idea how long that period of time will be or what we're ultimately supposed to do with it. When people ask, "What is my life's purpose?" what I think they're actually asking is, "What can I do with my life that will be important? What can I do with my life that will make a difference? What can I do with my life that I will find fulfilling and make me happy?" This is a much better place to start reflecting from as it takes you down a path of what you want to "do" rather than what you want to "be." Many people I speak to feel like they are not living according to a purpose because who they are "being" in life doesn't correlate to what they want to be "doing" in life.

So, how can you get to your purpose if you don't know yet what it is? Well, in reading and developing my own awareness in this critical element of the Code Block, I eventually settled on seven questions (the power of seven again!) that I hope can help you tap into your awareness. Clearly, I cannot even begin to help coach you on the answers, but some honest reflection and keeping notes of your responses to these seven key questions will help you begin to narrow down your thinking.

Please note that these questions are not numbered in any order of priority; some questions may resonate with you more than others, but hopefully a few of them will get you thinking. By the way, remember what I asked you to do in the introduction—be honest and true to yourself; you're not helping anyone, least of all yourself, by not being true to yourself here.

1. **What are your strongest talents, gifts, and skills that you have developed in your life so far?** Don't think about what others would say or what your boss would; what do you feel are your strongest qualities, and how do you feel when you are using and displaying them? We are often afraid to state what we believe we are good at for fear of ridicule. However, for this question, it's your honesty and response that matter the most.

2. **If you were told you had one year left to live, what would you choose to spend that year doing, and how would you want to be remembered?** Nobody likes thinking about death, and why would we, because it freaks us out! Imagine that you spent one year being the person you dreamed of being, doing the things you dreamed of doing. Just one year. What values would you want to live by? What would you want to do? What would your obituary say? What would people say about you and who you were?

3. **What makes you forget to eat, sleep, and 'poop'?** We have all had that experience in life when we get so wrapped up in

something that we suddenly realize time has flown by; we realize we have not eaten for hours, and yet it is not a problem as we were so engrossed in our task. What takes you to those moments and why? They tend to be so fulfilling that we forget about everything else, so what are they for you?

4. **What problem would you give anything to solve?** I don't mean inventing a toothbrush that tells your toaster to pop out the bread after it has been toasted to a set shade; I mean, real issues like how to cure a horrible disease; how to inspire inner city kids to believe they can thrive irrespective of their class; how to educate third-world children to chase their goals; or feed the billions of people that live on this little blue marble sustainable without destroying the planet; you know, the easy stuff! Is there a major problem or cause locally or nationally that you feel passionately about solving, supporting or addressing, and if so, what is it?

5. **What do colleagues, family, and friends seek you out for?** Reflect on this and identify what it is about you that people come to you for and why. Is it because of a skill, a quality you have, or your competence? There is often a clue here to help you define your purpose when considering why others turn to you to solve some common recurring problem, theme, or issue.

6. **What was your dream as a child?** What were you passionate about? This may sound like a strange question, but as kids, we were in tune with our hearts. We knew what we loved, and for the most part, we didn't care what people thought about it. We would openly express what we wanted to do "when we grew up," no matter how absurd or crazy it may have seemed. This question will point you toward a passion that you may have forgotten about.

7. **What is the dream or image you hold in your mind the most often when you allow yourself to daydream about your future?** It's the image or experience that you often find yourself wishing for that instantly feels right. It feels like it was destined to happen, and when you are daydreaming, it doesn't feel wrong or "not you"; it feels right.

Uncovering your purpose and passion in life is so much more than just what you will DO in this world. It is also about who you will BE, what you are committed to giving back, who you will help, and who you will be of service to. It is about getting off the couch and making a difference in other people's lives and being a part of something bigger than yourself. So be brave. Answer the questions, reflect on your answers and reactions, and then take some action to begin to define your purpose, understand your passion in life, career or both.

After completing this exercise, do you have a sense of what makes you fulfilled, enlightened, excited, energized at the thought of living it, achieving it, experiencing it day after day? If you do, then great; you will find these code-bytes helpful in confirming your thinking and defining your purpose with even greater clarity. If you don't yet fully understand your purpose in detail, then that's okay because about 99 percent of people are in the same place. Research suggests that no more than 10 percent of people have goals in life (far less than you would think, which is sad), but very few of those people who have goals are "underpinned," that is, set on the solid foundations that we call purpose. Just keep taking time to reflect, to revisit these seven questions or work through the following code-bytes. Not having a specific purpose will not prevent you from progressing successfully through the SUCCESS Code®, but it may help when you need willpower and determination to keep going, so do keep working on this task.

Code-byte 2B: Your Internal GPS

When you use the GPS in your car, you enter a zip or postal code or an address as the destination, and the GPS system takes over and begins to guides you there. Even if you take the occasional wrong turn, within a matter of seconds the system has calculated a new route that might take longer, might mean a few more miles to travel, but it is still homing in on your destination. That's what your purpose is when you find it. It is your internal GPS, and the more specific you can be (i.e. clarity), the better the directions will be, and the quicker the system can get you there. That's what the goals you will set later for yourself will all be about—they will equip and support you along the "route" that you will take to get to your destination eventually and successfully.

Remember my earlier point: *My* purpose is to "use my growing knowledge, insight, and experiences to help all people unlock the SUCCESS Code® to develop winners in life and business." This purpose fuels me, energizes me; I feel alive when I'm helping people. I passionately enjoy trying to inspire people to do the same and achieve success and fulfilment in life and business, and it's what I hope to spend the rest of my career doing. My *goals*, therefore, are simply *actions* to get me there: Write a chapter by X. Research a topic by Y. Prioritize my diary to spend time on Z. In future exercises that we focus on, such as the *DART-board Goal System toolkit* you will come across shortly, your purpose will be the foundation, the anchor point for many of the goals you will set for all aspects of your life. No matter how "lost" or distracted you may get at times, so long as your GPS system is still tracking to the set destination, you will continue to move towards it.

I have goals that focus on health and exercising every day. My goals focus on getting enough sleep. My goals focus on restricting alcohol (not completely!) each week. I have goals related to exercise, but the "purpose" or the zip code of this journey on the GPS is still crystal clear and doesn't change. That's how I want you to reflect here. Are you clear on the zip code you are feeding into your GPS for YOUR journey?

Code-byte 2C: Creating a Purpose Statement

You were born with your own GPS that tells you clearly when you are on or off-purpose simply judging by the amount of joy, happiness, and fulfilment in your life, your career or your profession at that point in time. They are sadly just fleeting moments, but when you talk and engage others about a particular subject, a subject that really interests you and lifts your mood and happiness when you do, you can lose track of time and you feel like you could talk for hours!

What was it about the subject matter that made you feel like that? So happy, enthused and energised? One answer could be that it was because the subject, topic or interest is close to your inner GPS, the internal desires and dreams that we all harbour deep within our hearts and souls, and maybe this conversation touched that desire, thereby making you feel more alive and animated than when holding a normal conversation. It could be a program on TV that just pricks your attention, and you listen and absorb every single word of it. It could be a magazine article you accidentally come across that just speaks to you in a way that is personal and deep. Figuring out what you want to do in life and then organising your life around the task of how you can make a living from doing it is the challenge that will help transform purpose into reality.

Here's one way to help you approach the task and help you write a few lines or a paragraph that may help you frame your purpose into a strong, powerful and personal purpose statement:

1. List **THREE** of your unique personal qualities (enthusiasm, drive, creativity, patience, or whatever describes you).

   _____ ; _____ ; _____

2. Now, list **TWO** ways you enjoy expressing or using these qualities when you interact with others (inspiring, informing, supporting, coaching, teaching, or whatever that describes you).

   _____ ; _____

3. Picture the world today in a perfect state of harmony. Everything is working perfectly right now. What does it feel like? How are you interacting with others? Write a short statement, in the present tense, describing this ultimate state, the perfect world as you see and feel it. Remember, a perfect world is a fun place to be (for example, in a perfect world, "Everyone is winning and achieving. Success and contentment are everywhere. Everyone is performing to their potential. Winners smile and succeed in life").

   _____

   _____

_____

_____

Now, combine your thoughts and words from points 1, 2, and 3 above into a single summary purpose statement (such as, "My purpose is to use my *enthusiasm, patience,* and *creativity* to *inspire* and *inform* as many children as possible *to maximize their potential and achieve success in life.*" This example came from a lady who was working in accounting but was never truly fulfilled until we captured her true purpose. She now teaches primary school children and has never been happier).

_____

_____

_____

_____

Once you have refined your "Purpose Statement" to something you can entirely buy into and that truly captures what you feel is true for you, read it every day at least twice a day. Add it to your *Code-Breaker Toolkit* when asked later and make time daily to sit and reflect on it for a few minutes. As we move forward through the later Blocks of the SUCCESS Code®, especially goal-setting systems, do try and ensure that they align with and serve to fulfil your purpose or the thing you are most passionate about in life, work or both.

Code-byte 2D: The Power of *If*

Another way to try and nail down your passion, your purpose in life, is by reflecting on your answers to a set of "If" scenarios. This is an exercise where you read each statement that all start with the word *if*, and then jot down your thoughts, responses, and reflections.

If you had all the money in the world, how would you spend your time?

If you could design your perfect day in detail, what would it look like?

If pressed for a quick response, what three activities set your soul on fire?

If you had the power to change your career tomorrow, what would you love to do for a living?

_____

_____

_____

_____

If you were ten years old again, what would you want to be when you grew up?

_____

_____

_____

_____

If pressed for a quick response, what did you love to do deep down before the world told you to become practical?

_____

_____

_____

_____

Hopefully, by taking some time to consider these "if" scenarios, you are able to get a stronger sense of what lies at your core. It may not come instantly or you may have known it all your life, you have just not yet had the compelling reason to take action.

Code-byte 2E: The Purpose Circles

Hopefully, the code-bytes above are helping you form a clearer view of your purpose and what your passion is for life or career or both. I hope you are starting to gain some clarity here, but it is fine if you are still unsure what this specifically means for you right now. Defining your purpose can at times be frustratingly elusive. It is like trying to remember a dream the next morning. The harder you try to force it back into your memory to see it again with complete clarity, the more abstract a concept it becomes. Sometimes, by trying to force it into the light, we inadvertently cast it in shadows. If, however, you are able to now state your purpose concisely and with clarity, it is true to you. Having this understanding and clarity is wonderful, but now you must start to centre this purpose in everything you do from this point forward.

The following diagram is a powerful but simple model that helps me understand the significance of purpose and the benefits for you and for others in finding it and living up to it.

Purpose Circles: Finding the "sweet spot" at the centre?

The Purpose Circles are excellent at bringing the importance of purpose, of defining your passion in life and seeking to put it at the centre of what you do. When you find your purpose in life, it will obviously be something you love to do. It is something that you are good at, and often, it is something the world (someone, somewhere) needs—a service, a product, your skills or expertise, or just your time. Then when you understand how you can earn a living from it, the circles join together and your real purpose and passion is effectively the "sweet spot" right at the centre where the four purpose circles overlap. It is your passion, your mission, and vocation, and therefore your profession.

Summary Reflection 1

Please do not make the mistake of assuming that your purpose will simply fall into your lap one Tuesday morning just because you read this chapter. I suspect that countless people live and exist in life without ever discovering what would have given their life meaning or without ever having the chance to even explore such a fundamental thing. Therefore, if you have the opportunity and ability to embark on this search, you should not squander that opportunity. It is within you, and if you know it and can see it in great clarity, that is wonderful. If it is not yet clear, take time to look for it. It is a task well worth exploring.

You will come to understand in the days, weeks, and maybe years ahead that a clarity of purpose in life and in the business world is a pretty unstoppable force when momentum is built. I mentioned it earlier; losing weight is never really a purpose, at best it is a goal. But losing weight to have more energy to play and to be a better parent, or to improve your life expectancy to be around for your grandchildren, now that is a purpose and passion! Starting a business that you have always wanted to do, moving to a new profession or career path that you know will fulfil you, these can become your purpose in life. Take the time to do the exercises if you need help to stimulate your thinking. If you know your purpose now, you probably have always known it. Is now the time when you finally decide to do something about it?

Summary Reflection 2

During a visit to the NASA Space and Rocket Centre in 1962, the US president at the time, John Kennedy, noticed a cleaner carrying a brush as he walked past. The president interrupted his tour, walked over to the man, and said, "Hi, I'm Jack Kennedy. What are you doing?" "Well, Mr. President," the cleaner responded, "I'm helping to put a man on the moon." For most people, the perception here was that this cleaner was just cleaning the building. However, on a personal and deep level, because of the larger story unfolding around him, in his mind, his purpose was in helping to make history. He was so purposeful in his ways that even the president of the United States was drawn to him and engaged him in a conversation.

Sticking to the topic of NASA, I want to use the rockets they launch as a wonderful metaphor for purpose. If you break it down, the rocket only ever has one purpose—to get to the moon, nowhere else, just the moon. Everything on the rocket, including the huge boosters that fire it up to the sky, are all designed for one purpose, getting the rocket to the moon. The astronauts on board the rocket have dials and information panels providing them with great detail about speed, trajectory, power, oxygen levels, and much more information. The job of the astronaut team is to make those minor adjustments as necessary to keep the rocket going in the right direction, toward the moon.

How clear are you on your mission to the moon? Yes, it is incredibly scary to even contemplate such a journey, and if you watch a rocket lifting off, you will notice the huge plumes of fire and rocket fuel that are required just to get the rocket a few feet off the ground. Then, as the power kicks in, the rocket begins to climb and climb, and eventually it is several miles high, breaking through the atmosphere and into space. It is the same for all of us when we start such a journey: The amount of effort and energy and willpower required to just get us started is massive. But once the first few steps have been taken, your rocket boosters (your goal systems in the next Code Block) will begin to do their job, and you will accelerate upward by the second...but we need to know our destination first.

As ever with the majority of people, staying on the ground and just watching is sadly enough for them. Ordinary will do, and while they may have once dreamed of being that astronaut, it is a dream that they have forgotten. So, what if you decide instead to go on this amazing, scary, but thrilling journey? What if you now decide to explore why you're here, discovering what you love to do, and how your unique gifts and talents can impact others for the better and leave a legacy that goes way beyond ordinary, average, and forgettable?

Of course, that second approach involves taking more perceived risk, but it also leads to incredibly rewarding opportunities and experiences. It means living a much bigger life story, one where your purpose matters, and where men end up on the moon as a result.

Summary Reflection 3

Doing what you love to do, what you were put on this earth to do, and often in the service to others, is the cornerstone of personal and professional happiness. Explore your feelings and passions in life and see where they take you. You may feel that life is okay right now. It is ticking along and things are alright, nothing out of the ordinary, just alright. However, life should and can be so much more than just alright.

Imagine a hose with water trickling out from the end. Yes, of course, water is coming out of the hose, but it is more of a trickle than a powerful surge. As you examine the hose, you notice a kink in it; it is slightly twisted. The moment you correct that kink, the force of the water coming out of the hose surges and becomes considerably more powerful. And this is just a result of correcting a minor kink in the rubber! Therefore, understand what you need to do to correct your kink in the hose and find your purpose and passion in life, and when you do, the power, fulfilment, and energy to drive you forward will be incredible.

*Compelling Action 2*_____

Update your *Code-Breaker Toolkit* sheet under Code Block 2. Now, please write your "Purpose Statement" as per code-byte 2C. Take time to reflect and consider but here you want to write down a statement that describes your main qualities, gifts and strengths. How you might express such qualities and the impact this will have on you, others, everyone!

_____

Code Block 3
Construct Goal Systems

"If you want to be happy, set a goal that commands your thoughts, liberates your energy and inspires your hopes."

– Andrew Carnegie

The combination lock is now beginning to turn. We have accepted "ownership" of our life in Code Block 1 and realized that our success in moving forward, personally or professionally, completely depends on us. It is our choices, decisions, and responses to those key moments and situations we face each day that decide our outcomes.

We are now progressing toward understanding our purpose and passion in Code Block 2, specifically the "thing we know we truly are about." Refining this in detail and with clarity is crucial in order to fuel our rocket, to propel us forward with excitement and passion, and to give us the energy and desire to keep pushing on when difficulties and challenges arise.

The next step in the code is Code Block 3: Construct Goal Systems. This is where we begin to move toward specific and focused action or actions. I want you to view the goal-setting and goal systems processes like an iceberg as shown in the rather basic figure provided below.

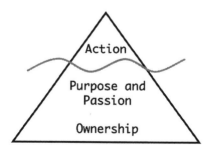

Iceberg Model: Ownership and Purpose is hidden below the surface while Action is what is visible to others

It is estimated that some 85 percent of any iceberg that you see floating in the sea is hidden below the surface; you cannot see most of it. The same is true for our goal systems. In the model above, it is the purpose you have clarified along with the ownership you have accepted for your future that make up the vast majority of the iceberg. The bit that everyone sees above the surface is the doing part, the productivity. What you do here is visible, it is public, it is the crucial activity of taking action, but the greater mass holding up the iceberg under the water are the powerful components of purpose and ownership.

In many books and theories on building for personal success and achievement either in your personal life or business, the dominant strategy suggested is almost always some form of goal setting. That is not a bad thing by the way; any teaching, lesson, or suggestion to set goals in your life or in business is recommended. However, in my opinion and experience, setting goals in isolation of anything else means there are just too many risks in achieving the positive intention behind the goals themselves. You need to get your "inner foundations" right to build the goal systems upon, and that is why we spent time on the previous two Code Blocks, "Ownership" and "Purpose," to obtain these foundations. Even with this point in mind about goal setting, I'm going to challenge another aspect behind the conventional goal-setting systems or techniques that you may be familiar with from past experiences. Your success, growth and achievement from goal setting are just as much about the SYSTEM as it is about the goal.

Of course, it is vital that we have a set of specific goals to aim for. Goals allow us to create our future in advance and enable us to get what we want. They allow us to envision our destiny, and, in turn, shape our lives. They give us direction and hope. This is the power of goals. But I firmly believe that without the right systems underpinning your goals, you are going to struggle to sustain progress. There is a significant and fundamental difference between goals and systems. *Goals* are the results you want, the outcomes you desire (run a marathon, lose twenty pounds, start a business, become a millionaire, get promoted), but it is the *systems* that underpin progress toward these goals, and therefore are equally as important as the goals themselves.

Let me try and explain this better. In professional sports, the goal of several leading teams is to win the championship every season. To do that, they will no doubt have systems in place on player recruitment, training, nutrition, recovery, tactics, player rotation, strategies, and many more systems I suspect. Now, all teams know that there can only be one champion team, and yet they share the same goal. I would argue that the team with the best and most consistent systems over a season will win the championship and perhaps go on and contend for several successive championships if these systems are regularly monitored, refined, and improved. Having a goal is essential as we need to know where we are headed but having supporting and specific systems and processes underpinning the goal are equally as vital to our overall success. In this example, both winners and losers share the same goal (as do the athletes who all set the goal of winning the Olympic gold medal, or the job applicants who all set the same goal to get that one job offer), but it will be the athletes and applicants with the most consistent and focused systems who are most likely to succeed over a period.

To reinforce this point, a *goal* is often defined as a single moment in time, but what happens when you achieve it? Of course, the joy and satisfaction of achieving a goal are amazing, fulfilling, and must not be discounted, but what then? For example, let's assume running the marathon is your goal. You finish running twenty-six miles; you're tired and exhausted but elated and euphoric at the same time. But would you completely stop the training and following the nutrition plan that got you to run the marathon now that your goal has been accomplished? Do you revert to your old lifestyle and quickly lose those fitness and diet habits that made you so healthy just because that specific goal was achieved? Develop great systems, and the goals will take care of themselves.

Or, let's assume you set a goal to become the top sales performer in your organisation. You build systems to get you there (more appointments with clients, more proposals issued, better product knowledge, improved closing skills, and so on). Such systems will make a big difference and could well be the basis for your goal success. You get there but what then; do you stop seeing clients, stop learning, stop closing, and stop earning the biggest bonuses? Unlikely! You have built systems that allow you to have continued success and achievement, so you set other, even bigger goals and have confidence that you know you can do it.

When I tell my kids to tidy up their bedroom usually as part of earning their weekly allowance, they rush around to achieve this goal and put stuff away to create the illusion of tidiness. However, within a few hours of receiving their allowance, the room is a mess again because they do not have a system to support their goal. This is what I call a "trampoline goal"; you bounce up and down, high and low, between the goal itself and the system underpinning it, whether good or bad.

In this step of the SUCCESS Code®, the code-bytes ask you to consider systems as important as the goals themselves. If you have set goals for yourself in the past and failed, it wasn't your fault. Don't blame yourself. It's the fault of the system you had or did not have. In my opinion, we do not rise to the level of our goals; we fall to the level of our systems, which are intended to drive us to achieve our goals. If we have aspiring goals AND great systems underpinning them, then amazing things can and will occur, and that is what we are going to develop in this Code Block.

So, now we need specific goals that will help us move toward success, achievement, and personal or professional fulfilment, and I have developed a process over the years for this purpose; we will use it for this Code Block. Experts on the science of success know that the brain is basically a goal-seeking organism. Whatever goals you assign to your subconscious mind, it will work night and day to achieve them, and there are countless case studies to support the power of goal setting.

In this Code Block, we are going to take some time to consider where we are in life in all those key areas that matter (health, career, friendships, relationships, finances), and we will set goal systems to get us where we want to go. We create our destiny and move toward our future. Goal setting and attainment is the most powerful method of doing this. Now, I know in life we focus a lot on goals and goal setting, creating a real danger of goal overwhelm. People can stop believing in their goals or simply not buy into them because of the fear of goal fatigue that is attached to the subject. Do not let that be you. Your goals, when you have them, are yours and only yours, and when you build the systems to deliver them, goal fatigue will not become a factor here.

What follows are five code-bytes to consider regarding your understanding or approach to goal systems. Consider and reflect upon each one in turn, taking the required action or actions that you feel are most appropriate to your situation or challenge.

Code-byte 3A: Understanding the Power of Goals

When you take the time to consider and then set goals and the systems to enable them, you begin to set up your thinking, actions, and mind-set in such a way as to squeeze the most you can from every situation, opportunity, or moment. There's so much to experience and enjoy in life, so many wonderful things we can all have, but they won't just be put on a plate for you.

Unfortunately, you are going to have to work hard for them and earn them. The great news, however, is that following a good goal-setting program or methodology is going to be incredibly beneficial in getting you there. As I have said earlier, this is the stage in the SUCCESS Code® where "doing" becomes essential. It's the part of the iceberg that others will see. There's no substitute or silver bullet here; it's going to take effort, but this effort is important and so worth it.

Take a moment and imagine you're on vacation somewhere across the globe. You typically only have a week or so to take in the sights, sounds, and experiences of the destination that you have imagined. Now, with such limited time, would you not make some form of plan for each day? On day one, we will go here. On day two, we will spend the day doing this. On day three, we will go here, and so on. Or would you leave your hotel every morning and just decide to turn left or right at the front door and leave it to *luck* to take you to the sights and destinations you want to visit?

Well, on many levels, our lives can be like one big unplanned vacation. You and I have limited time; it's called *living*, and our goal is to identify and chase the dreams, experiences, and desires that we want to get the most out of our "vacation," our lives. To do this, we have to know specifically what we want to do and ideally in great detail. That's where the power of goal setting comes in, and I have tried to share the five most powerful reasons behind goal setting and goal systems to get you fired up and ready to set and build your own!

1. **Goals propel you forward.** Writing down a goal with a set date for to accomplish it gives you something to plan and work for. A written goal is an external representation of your inner desires, and it is a constant reminder of what you need to accomplish. There's a very common pattern that comes with working toward goals that we're all familiar with: You set your mind to something, you get excited and work like mad, and then your motivation starts to wane. Having goals that you can focus on and visualize helps you better connect yourself with your inner desires and gives you the motivational energy you need to work through periods where your focus inevitably starts to wane.

2. **Goals turn insurmountable mountains into walkable hills.** Most of us have big dreams that seem impossible to accomplish. It's easy to feel discouraged when you're staring at a massive, seemingly insurmountable mountain. Proper goal setting can help break larger, intimidating aspirations into smaller, more achievable stepping stones. Planning toward these smaller goals not only makes it easier to formulate a definite plan of action that we can start working on right away but research has also shown that hitting smaller milestones provides real motivation and greater contentment. You can take this lesson and apply it to your own life. Take the mountains you need to climb and break them up into smaller hills that you can walk. You'll be happier and more motivated to start working toward that next milestone on your way to greatness.

3. **Goals help us believe in ourselves.** Setting goals for yourself is a way to fuel your ambition. Goal setting isn't just about creating a plan for your life and holding yourself accountable; it's also about giving yourself the inspiration that is necessary to aim for things

you never thought were possible. Do you want to accomplish something that many people dream about but few people ever actually accomplish? Unless you make it a goal for yourself and work every day toward achieving it, why would you ever believe that you could accomplish it? Unless you see yourself slowly making progress, your dreams and aspirations are nothing more than vague notions floating around in your imagination.

4. **Goals hold you accountable for failure.** If you don't write down concrete goals and give yourself a time line for achievement, how can you look back and re-evaluate your path if you fail? There's something extremely humbling about looking back on a goal you set for yourself six months, one year, or even five years ago and realizing that you were supposed to accomplish a lot more than you actually have. It is a concrete sign that whatever you're doing isn't working, and you need to make real changes if you want to get where you want to be.

5. **Goals tell you what you truly want.** There are certainly times when we set goals that don't really reflect what we want. Sometimes, we think we need more money when what we really need is a change of environment or someone to love. Sometimes, we think we want more free time, but what we really want is work that we can truly be passionate about. Sometimes, we think we want to be alone, but we really need to be around more positive people. If you never set goals in the first place, how do you find out what you truly want? If you wander through life with vague notions of "success" and "accomplishment," you might never discover that buying a new BMW isn't what will bring you true happiness or that landing that coveted promotion at work will make you miserable because the extra money and fancy title won't make up for the reduced time with your family.

Hopefully, these five key points have helped solidify in your own mind the importance and power of goal setting, so in the next code-byte that follows, we begin to understand and use a system to help us identify and nail down the goals most important to us.

Code-byte 3B: *DART-board Goal System toolkit*

I have mentioned this over and over again: Even having basic goals is hugely more beneficial than having none. "I want to be a millionaire" or "I want to be top salesperson this quarter" or "I want to lose twenty pounds" or "I want to run my own business" are all positive goals to have, and in all these examples, there is at least a destination. You have an end point; at least you know "where" you are going. If you write these goals down, then it will be even better! Committing to writing your goals down on paper will help your focus and sub-conscious mind understand the destination even more than by just saying it. In Code Blocks 1 and 2, you spent time understanding that ownership of your life and what comes next is entirely dependent on you. You should also be clear on what you feel your purpose in life is. What is it that will make you happy, fulfilled, and fuel you for the journey ahead? That journey is the rest of your life!

Now in this code-byte, you are going to take time and space to review all the key elements of your life, eight areas in fact, and by using the *DART-board Goal System toolkit* that I use. You are going to make a **D**ecisive **A**ssessment of the **R**eal **T**hemes in your life, hence the DART acronym. It is extremely important that you complete this exercise as honestly and openly as you can. You will need to download the *DART-board Goal System* toolkit from the "Resources" section at www.unlockthecode. co.uk to do this. Please do so!

Now at this stage, I am only looking for you to complete part 1 of the *DART-board Goal System toolkit* and to take some time to reflect on each of these eight categories on the "DART-board." There are questions in the *DART-board Goal System toolkit* to work through that will help you form a view of how you assess the key aspects of your life at this point. Your responses here will help you see clearly where the focus of your subsequent goals should be. An overview of the "DART-board" is on the following page.

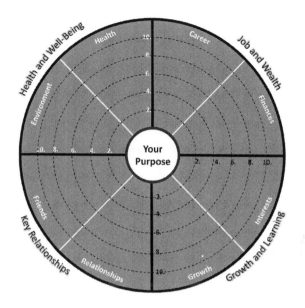

DART-board Goal System toolkit: To assess the current position across your whole life

In this critical exercise, you evaluate all eight aspects of the board and form a view, an opinion, or an assessment of how each of these eight categories currently plays out in your life. The questions and prompts in the toolkit will help you form that view. You will be required to score yourself from zero to ten based on how happy, fulfilled, contented, and satisfied you are within each category at this point in your life.

Upon assessing each of the eight categories, you will then map out the picture as described in the toolkit to "see" your life today in terms of your assessment of all eight categories. It will then become visibly clear where the focus of your goal setting should be. Doing this exercise for the first time can be quite emotional as you take time to reflect and score your satisfaction with pretty much everything that matters in your life. Emotion is good, by the way, because it usually leads to taking action. Right at the heart of the word *emotion* is the word *motion*—doing something, moving forward. That is the power of the *DART-board Goal System toolkit*.

After assessing all eight areas, we move from there into part 2 and narrow in on your "Deliberate Dozen Goals." Again, please refer to the *DART-board Goal System toolkit* and work through the process methodically as instructed. It is sometimes not easy to prioritize your goals especially if you feel everything is very important, but we cannot possibly manage twenty, thirty, forty, or more goals at once. We need to work through to find the most appropriate focus areas for us from the four main segments of the board (Health and Well-Being, Job and Wealth, Growth and Learning, Key Relationships) and build up a plan from there. Don't worry if you feel you are ignoring key areas that you really feel you want to include but cannot find space for. One of the many benefits of this process is that it is fluid. As one goal is achieved—and it will be—one more is added. The *DART-board Goal System toolkit* is something you will return to often, at least three or four times a year, to add new goals or change or remove pre-existing ones as you move forward in your life on this new path.

Eventually, with a bit of time, space, and reflection, you will form your "Deliberate Dozen Goals" in part 2 of the *DART-board Goal System toolkit,* and this will typically be split into short, mid and long-term time frames. You will have the *why* aligned with each goal, and the *DART-board Goal System toolkit* tells you to stop at this point and return to this part of the book because of the significance of the next code-byte, your goal SYSTEMS.

Code-byte 3C: System Support

I stated at the beginning of this chapter that the systems you have to support the achievement of your goals are equally as important as the goals themselves. I cannot stress this enough. You ideally need to know your "why" (your purpose) as this is crucial, but so is the system you build to enable the goal. Let me try and further explain this important point.

Imagine that you have worked through the *DART-board Goal System toolkit* and prioritized a mid-term goal under "Health and Well-being."

The goal: You want to complete a 10K run by a set date. It is a great goal, specific and personal to you, and you have it as one of your "Deliberate Dozen" in the toolkit. Now, the goal, as I have said, is great, but achieving the goal is going to be about the systems you build to help you get there. It is thinking about the days you know you can do the training runs. What will need to change or be moved to ensure the set training runs are completed within your schedule and nailed down? It is the diet plan and when and what you will eat in specific terms to help you succeed in your training runs. It is the friend or training partner you identify to run with who will be a great motivating factor, but you need to agree on a plan and timetable (a system) for when you can both get to the park for a run.

Now, imagine setting a goal to getting promoted to a specific job that you aspire to. Again, the goal works for you because it is specific, and you know it is important to you because you have prioritized it into your "Deliberate Dozen." Let's ensure, therefore, that we build a system to underpin success. Who will you ask to mentor and coach you to improve? When and how frequently will you meet? What skills or competencies do you need to improve to progress? What training courses, books, or learning do you need to address that gap? Which days and what time will you set aside for learning and developing? Which executives or managers in the company will be influential in this goal being realized? What is your plan (system) to speak and engage with these people on a frequent basis to raise your profile, share your goals, and seek feedback on the actions or steps necessary?

I hope the previous examples help you understand the importance of this code-byte in systemizing your goal setting and therefore significantly improving your chances of success. I want you to be excited and enthused by the key point you have just grasped. Only a very small percentage of the population has goals. Even less have them written down, and even less have thoughtfully built systems to ensure success and only a tiny proportion have "ownership and purpose" clear and aligned in their thinking! You should now be in this small percentage, and when you consider your understanding of Code Blocks 1 and 2, you are establishing a platform for the most amazing progress and success in your life. Don't waste it.

I want you to now return to part 3 of the *DART-board Goal System toolkit* and take the time to build your "system" for each of the "Deliberate Dozen" goals that you have settled on. Be specific and think before you commit to any process or action in your system. Is this going to be achievable? What factors (distractions, existing commitments, or habits) do you need to break, consider, or overcome?

At the end of this Code-Bye, you should now have fully completed the *DART-board Goal System toolkit*. You will have scored yourself on all eight aspects of your life, prioritized your "Deliberate Dozen," and, preferably, have a mix of short-term, mid-term, and long-term goals. If they are in some way aligned to your purpose in life, the place or goal in your heart that you feel will make you most fulfilled in life, then even better! The final stage included building specific systems to ensure you have the platform to go ahead and do it.

In the next few code-bytes within this Code Block, I am going to highlight a number of techniques or practices that will help you in the days and weeks ahead as you begin the task of taking action, the doing, the motion. This is where the magic truly starts to happen.

Code-byte 3D: The Importance of the Block Schedule

As you proceed from the previous code-bytes, and if you are like everyone who starts this journey, you will soon be in danger of feeling overwhelmed. You may have your "Deliberate Dozen," but with perhaps two or three actions in each of your goal systems, you can quickly feel swamped with the scale of the task, and this is often when people quit. All the great work, the absolute foundations of success and achievement have been set, but when the first real test presents itself, people can quickly lose control and momentum and walk away. Do not let this be you! In the current technological space we all live in, there is NO WAY that this should happen to you, but in case it does, *block scheduling* is one of the ways to help you overcome this challenge.

Pretty much all of us nowadays possess a gadget of some sort (phone, tablet, PC, etc.) that contains a diary or calendar feature or application. This is your new best friend. If you don't have a gadget of any type, go to the local store and buy a cheap diary. You need something. The point I am making in this code-byte is that if something so vital to your success and goal achievement is not on your calendar, in your schedule or diary, it will simply not happen. If the systems have not been established to the level you need them to be, the chances of your achieving your goals will be considerably less. It has to be in the schedule. If the essential activities within your goal system are not scheduled, it really is a flawed system. If there's nothing in your calendar to drive you forward and tell you the "what to do" and "when to do it," you are not optimally setting up your systems to deliver your goals. The sense of clarity and urgency that comes with block scheduling is an excellent way to keep you on track.

Over the years, I have learned and developed my own block scheduling process that I now feel works for me, and as I don't want you to go through the same mistakes and frustrations as I did, here's my top-five tips for effective block scheduling. I tend to block schedule at the start of every month, but you can do this weekly, even daily if it helps, but I typically find by block scheduling weekly or monthly, you tend to see the bigger picture and can schedule more sensibly.

Looking at the month ahead of you:

1. **Weekly Review Block.** This is a fifteen-minute block that I schedule every Sunday morning. I take time to assess progress by comparing my progress with the past week's block schedule to ensure that any lessons or mistakes from the past week are reflected in any fine-tuning I make in the week ahead. I also check that nothing unplanned has entered my schedule and compromised the blocks in place.

2. **Daily Refresh Block.** A ten-minute block every day, usually around 7 a.m. for me, to take a quiet moment and remind myself of my purpose, goals, and vision cards (more on this in the next code-byte), and this acts as an essential daily booster, reminding me of the "whys." I have even recorded this information on my

phone so that when I am sitting on a train, or running at the gym, or even driving the car, I can listen and reflect daily about the opportunity of the day ahead no matter where I am at that time.

3. **Family Block.** It is very important that I schedule time for my family in my diary. If my children have events at school or significant moments involving their hobbies and interests, or if we have important dates set as a family, they are blocked out, and I let nothing interfere with this. In terms of your own family and relationships, do look to block schedule time here and stick to it. It is important.

4. **Goal System Blocks.** The final element of the block schedule process involves the daily, weekly, or whatever frequency actions that your goal systems require. These MUST be in your schedule each month. Take time to think about them. I also look to try and combine systems within block schedules if possible. For example, if I have a health-related goal and the system involves exercising, then I will often use the same time to listen to a specific article or blog that I have as part of my systems for achieving a goal under personal growth. If you can work on two systems at once, do it!

5. **Blocker Hijackers.** Be wary of those people, colleagues, gadgets, or distractions that can disrupt the best laid-out schedules. Remove all temptations and distractions by turning things off or putting things away. When others try to hijack your schedule, in almost every instance I have found they can wait until my goal system schedule allows it.

Using these block-scheduling tips, I am able to schedule everything I need to do over the next week or month to ensure I am progressing in terms of everything I have in my "Deliberate Dozen," and I have essential systems underpinning these. I am able to make scheduling decisions on short-, mid-, and long-term goals and have set times each day and week to assess progress, maintain them the next day or week, and if necessary, refine them to get the maximum I can from the day or week ahead. It doesn't matter what system you choose for yourself, but please ensure you have one. Unless your actions and systems have been written down in your diary and scheduled, you will be leaving success to chance, and why would you ever choose to do that?

Code-byte 3E: Repetition Is the Mother of Skill

Typically, in the majority of goal systems, there are several tasks or actions that you have identified as crucial to the attainment of a goal. These are actions that you have deemed as vitally important and often needed to be performed every day, perhaps weekly, but certainly at a regular and repetitive frequency. The aim here is developing a *habit*. The focus is on repeating the activity until it becomes a *skill*.

Plenty of research has been conducted on how a habit has an enormous influence on your life, and several good books of late have been written on the subject. For example, did you know that about half of the decisions you think you make each day are actually habitual? You are not really deciding at all. Your brain is automatically programmed with the habit, so it is effectively making that decision for you. You don't really decide to brush your teeth every morning or check your mobile phone for updates before breakfast or put your seatbelt on when driving. They are habits you have developed. You probably have several more that you do automatically; I know I have. So, when you can apply the formula of developing a positive habit to those areas of your life where you need to, such as aspects of your goal systems, you will be amazed at what you can achieve in such a short period of time without even thinking too much about it.

The secret, therefore, is in understanding the simple, repeatable disciplines or actions that, when applied often, form incredibly powerful habits and can deliver transformational change in whatever aspects of your life you desire. I know it's much more "sexy and inspiring" to make dramatic proclamations of your path to millionaire status in a year or less, but the big goals you seek are usually somewhat different from the smaller, repeatable disciplines and habits that will get you there. Understanding this as you go about your daily actions required by your goal systems will help keep you moving forward.

The good news is that these small, crucial disciplines are often easy to do and therefore easy to develop into habits. Once you form a habit, like brushing your teeth or wearing a seatbelt, it manifests itself every time and will push you to amazing success. It's the compounding effect of doing the same positive task day-in, day-out that has the incredible effect I'm describing here. As the great Jim Rohn once said, "Systems and habit are the bridge between your goals and actually accomplishing them." Revisit the "Foundational Themes" section on habits at the beginning of this book if you need to. Building positive habits significantly helps you as you pursue and execute your goals based on the systems you have built to get you there.

Summary Reflection 1

Goals give us direction in life. They allow us to "set the future" the way we want it to be. Everyone needs a sense of purpose in their lives, and setting goals is a great way to identify your purpose and align with it. As the saying goes, "If you don't know where you're going, then you'll end up somewhere else."

Often without goals, you simply become a tool to help other people obtain theirs. Without goals, your life can feel like a boat that's floating aimlessly down a river. Setting goals is like getting paddles for your boat. You now have some control over which way you go and how you get there; this also makes you more positive. You have a sense of purpose, you're controlling your future, you're focusing on what's important, you're more motivated, you're starting to see results, and you're making better use of your time. All those things add up and help build a more positive attitude, which drives even more success. So, invest the time to set the right goals in the priority areas of your life and go achieve them.

Summary Reflection 2

An exercise or a reflective task that always disturbs me and those who do the exercise—in a positive and inspiring way I should add—is what I call the Rocking Chair moment. I want you to look at your "Deliberate Dozen Goals" and the systems you have built to enable them. These should all be on your completed *DART-board Goal System toolkit*. Read through each goal quietly and then imagine how you will feel having accomplished each of them. Visualize yourself achieving them, sense how you will feel, look, be, and so on. For five to ten minutes, using your imagination, put yourself there to sense how you will feel when, not if, the goals are achieved. You should feel positive, excited, and enthused to push forward to ensure that such images and feelings turn into reality.

Now I want you to imagine a different scenario, and this time, we are many years in the future. Let's imagine you are in your eighties, nineties, maybe even older, sitting in a rocking chair, reflecting on your life as you enter the final years of your life. How will you feel? Will you be reflecting on a life of happiness, fulfilment, and success, a life where you took ownership of what you wanted, and you set goals and went out and got them? You set more and more goals throughout your life and went on and built success and achievement for you and your family for many years to follow. You now sit here in the rocking chair with little to no regrets, knowing you have lived the life you wanted, and you feel happy and content with that.

Or, do you see yourself in the rocking chair frustrated and angry that you never went for it? There was always a reason why you did not, always something to get in the way and blame, and now that your time is almost up, you have unfulfilled dreams, goals, and aspirations, but the chance to fix the problem has now passed. But you have the tools now to ensure that when you are imagining yourself in that rocking chair, it is the first scenario I painted –positive and filled with no regrets. This is your life. Nobody else is going to live it for you, so why would you not go for it?

Summary Reflection 3

In Bronnie Ware's book, *Lessons from the Dying*, published in 2009, the single biggest reflections of those at the very end of life was, "I wish I'd had the courage to live a life true to myself, not the life others expected of me" and "I wish that I had let myself be happier." These were the most common regrets of all. When people realize that their lives are almost over and look back clearly on them, it is easy for them to see how many of their dreams and goals have gone unfulfilled.

Most people have died without even having chased half of their dreams or pursued a fraction of their goals, and they had to approach the end of their lives knowing that it was because of choices they had made or not made. Many did not realize until the end that the goal of happiness is a choice. They had stayed stuck in old patterns and poor habits. They chose mindless TV over reading a book. They chose ordinary and safety over extra-ordinary and excitement. The so-called comfort of familiarity overflowed into their lives, making goal setting rare. Fear of change had them pretending to others, and to themselves, that they were content, when deep within they longed to have pursued a different path by setting goals for a life of personal achievement, happiness, and fulfilment.

The life you have today and tomorrow is a *choice*. It is YOUR life. Choose consciously, choose wisely, and choose honestly. Choose *happiness*, and then build the goals and systems to get you there.

*Compelling Action 3*_____

Update your *Code-Breaker Toolkit* sheet under Code Block 3. You must enter your "Deliberate Dozen" goals and plan on when and how you will remind yourself of them. You should read through them every day and 'imagine' how you will feel when each of them is achieved. The systems and how you plan to achieve them are captured in the DART-board and Goal Assessment toolkit.

_____

Code Block 4
Commence Taking Action Today!

"Take action! An inch of movement will bring you closer to your goals than a mile of intention."

– Dr Steve Maraboli

Now that we have understood ownership of outcome and clarity of purpose and built goal systems to drive us forward, let's look at taking action. Unfortunately, the world does not pay you for what you know: Your value lies in what you do with what you know. One of the fundamental principles that I covered right at the beginning of the book was that knowledge alone is not power, in my opinion; it's what you do with the knowledge that creates the power, the momentum, and the life-changing outcomes that I know you want to have. Sadly, but not surprisingly, too many people get bogged down while analysing, planning, and preparing for the most amazing changes they want in their lives. While this is important, and we have done this in the earlier Code Blocks, what they really need to do is perhaps analyse less and start taking action!

When you take action in your life, you trigger all kinds of forces that will inevitably propel you toward success. You start to notice that you are serious in your intentions. People with similar goals begin to align themselves with you and offers of help and support begin to "just happen." You learn things about yourself from your journey that cannot be learned simply by listening to others or reading books. You get feedback on how to progress toward your goals and build better systems more efficiently and quickly. You attract people into your life who will support and encourage you, and all manner of good things begin to flow in your direction…but only once you begin to take ACTION.

In a business context and throughout my career, I have sat in several incredibly inspiring planning sessions or impactful strategy reviews when the level of thinking, ideas, and concepts to consider have been mind-blowing. The level of detail and scale of ideas and actions proposed were staggering, and if we had ever implemented or taken action on just half of them, we would have performed business miracles! You see, that's the issue in business and life at this stage of the SUCCESS Code®. You have fired up your personal ownership, you have fuelled your drive with purpose, and built twelve superb goals with systems that will guarantee success, but until you take action, they are never, ever going to deliver you the outcomes you truly want.

Let me be candid in this Code Block. In all of my time teaching and coaching people both in business and personal development, the one thing that ALWAYS seems to separate those we call winners from those we call losers is that winners take action. They simply get up and do what needs to be done to achieve their goals, and they are driven by a compelling purpose or vision. Everyone enjoys dreaming and setting goals. It's exciting to sit and write down all the things you want from your life—money, wealth, health, love, experiences, growth, family, and so on. Having such a view of your life and the direction you want to go is critical. However, once you have set that destination, you will never get closer to it until you take the first step or make the first call or read the first page. Taking action is now your focus.

More often than not, success, achievement, or personal happiness begins when you lean into it and open yourself up to opportunities and become willing to do whatever it takes to pursue your goals. Once you begin to take action and lean into it, you will begin to feel like you have control over your destiny and the outcomes and results you want. Making the choice to take action on one, some, or all of your goal systems is when you truly begin to take complete ownership of the rest of your life. You will be amazed at what begins to occur once positive intention moves to focused action, which hopefully develops into positive habit.

Thus, this next Code Block walks you through several code-bytes designed to help you focus on taking action. I also discuss their critical importance in terms of your happiness, success, and achievement. You may recall in the "Foundational Themes" chapter at the beginning of this book, I discussed the "easy-ness conundrum." Never has this principle been more applicable than now. You now understand the actions required to deliver on your goal systems, and frankly, I imagine they in and of themselves are easy to do. You know what's coming, though. You will have countless temptations and distractions that will also make it seem "easy" *not* to take action. Your future success and achievement are entirely dependent on how you address this conundrum.

Take action, because success demands taking action!

Code-byte 4A: The Self-Parenting Scenario

As much as I want and as desperate as I am to help you, I can't make you do this. It has to come from within you. Throughout our lives, particularly when we were children, we had parents, teachers, or guardians who typically made decisions for us. They told us when to do what. Our days were often structured from waking to going to sleep, and when it came to key moments of decision making, our parents or guardians would take over.

However, assuming that those of you reading this book today are at an age where you have some degree of responsibility for your own decisions when it comes to taking the actions required to achieve your goals, how you "self-parent" matters the most. Nobody is going to make you do these actions; it's got to be you and only you. Of course, you can always seek help and support from coaches and mentors and explore examples of people who have succeeded and what and how they did so. But in the end, it will almost always come down to the choice of taking action based on the advice and support you receive. You have to parent yourself and ensure action is taken.

Remember the formula from Code Block 1: Your outcomes and results are entirely based on your decisions and choices in those specific moments of time. Consider that every action ever taken in the world was "fathered" by the decision of whether or not to do something. One of my own reflections when developing this code-byte, thinking back to my childhood, was my fondness for "excuse-itis." I was wonderfully creative as a child coming up with reasons not to do something my parents asked of me when I didn't want to do it. I often came up with five or six excuses to wriggle out of doing homework. You will recall the result was the first brown envelope! I did not want to shop for new school shoes, so I developed excuses to avoid the task. I never wanted to do the chores I was asked to do, so I spent more time making up excuses to get out of doing them than the chores would have taken if I had just done them! In these instances, my parents often would over-rule and I was made to do what they wanted, but as an adult such moments present themselves every single day, and without parental overruling, who is going to make things happen? You, and only you.

Let me cover one theme I hear about too often when it comes to reasons not to take action, and that is the subject of health. Again, referring to my own childhood, many of my excuses to avoid taking action were based on health. "I can't do that because I have a cold, a sore knee, pain in my back, a headache." Rarely if ever did that work with my parents, and even if there were some truth in my excuse, and I did perhaps have a headache or a sore knee, I was still made to do or complete whatever action they had asked me to do. This code-byte is not intended to suggest that those with serious illnesses or chronic health challenges should be dismissed, and self-parenting should apply in this case. Instead, this code-byte applies to the vast majority of us who find health reasons or excuses to avoid most of the actions we need to take, especially when these actions are linked to goals related to health, fitness, or lifestyle.

Stop listening to yourself about these aches, pains, and groans that you feel like you want to use as excuses. The more you talk to yourself about an ailment, a problem, or even a common cold, the worse it seems to get! Talking about how sore your ankle is or that you have a cold so you can't start your actions until tomorrow—which never comes because you will find another excuse tomorrow—is like adding fertilizer to weeds! The weeds will grow, and you will give yourself a superpower to come up with even better excuses day after day after day!

I am sure you can consider a whole host of so-called reasons or excuses to find ways of avoiding action. Time. Age. Priorities. Work stuff. Home stuff. Family stuff. Other stuff...and on it goes. When you find yourself straying into excuse-itis, quickly go back and recall your decision at the start of the SUCCESS Code® to own your life and what is going to happen from today. Understand your why, your purpose, and so on, and why you want to change, improve, develop, succeed. Remind yourself that you now have goals and supporting systems to help you get there, so the only thing you need to do now is take action, of any shape or form; just take that first step.

This is all the more important when there's nobody to parent you to encourage you to take action. Look for the reasons why you can do it and not excuses why you can't. I can't make you take these actions—nobody can in reality. This has to come from you, but take comfort that once the action happens, so does momentum, and progress follows soon after!

Code-byte 4B: Action–Progress Loop

I like the power of this model as well as the simple yet profound theory behind it. It helps me understand the power that even the smallest bit of effort or action can have when I'm unsure, uncertain, or procrastinating about taking action on any of my goal systems. As you can see in the diagram below, the loop is continual. Once the loop begins from step 1, it becomes self-propelling, and I can testify to its power from experiencing it hundreds of times in my own life.

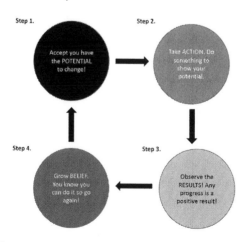

Potential Loop: Taking potential to action and then belief

Step 1 of the figure states that you should acknowledge that you have the ability and POTENTIAL to change. That is not up for debate here. You know you can do it. Whatever the action (step 2), you have the potential to do it. Knowing you can means that taking ACTION or not is now entirely your choice, and that forms step 2. However, when you do take action, you will start to see RESULTS, moving toward step 3. The results or outcomes may be big or small, but this does not matter. What matters is that you see the tiniest bit of progress, which fuels BELIEF (step 4), and you begin to appreciate that you have the potential to do more, and so the loop goes around again. This is the loop that drives someone from being a couch-potato to completing a 10K run. It drives people from moving from a job they dislike to a job they adore. This loop supports someone who wants to meet new friends or form new relationships.

All results and progress breed confidence and in turn fuel belief, reinforcing your understanding of just how much potential you have to achieve this goal. Momentum is built, and once this happens, it is arguably unstoppable. The analogy of a steam train is applicable here. A steam train moves forward ever so slowly once the power of the coal systems in the engines starts kicking in. In those first few yards of progress, even a tiny little pebble on the track can stop the steam train from progressing because it has not yet gained enough momentum to run over the pebble. However, once it builds up a certain degree of power and consequently speed, it is unstoppable. A fully powered steam train can crash through most things, as will you, once you begin to understand the power of taking action and apply it to your future success, happiness, and progress.

Code-byte 4C: The Procrastination Problem

Overthinking your actions, overanalysing your goal systems, or simply waiting for the "perfect" moment to take action is a total success killer! Procrastination is one of the biggest challenges you face when putting your goals and plans into action. It is a challenge we all frequently encounter.

For me, procrastination is the preference of carrying out far less important tasks or actions or irrelevant "stuff" instead of more urgent and critical tasks. It can also be seen as the choice to indulge in "easier" actions instead of "harder" ones, and as a consequence, putting off crucial actions or tasks for a later time. Procrastination is that gap between the intention of doing something you know you need to do and the actual doing of it, or not! It is when that gap changes from seconds to minutes, hours, and days, and then perhaps never, that the problem has a huge impact on your potential to achieve, succeed, and do the things you need to do to achieve your goal systems.

I won't use this code-byte to reflect on the significance of time, specifically wasted and unproductive time, for your future success. There are countless articles and helpful sites all over the internet focussing on the procrastination problem. If this is a real issue for you, take some time to understand the problem and try to deal with it. It is more harmful to your achievement and success than I am highlighting here. Considering the significance of the phrase, "Success demands taking action," do not allow procrastination to hold you up any longer than it should.

I have struggled with this problem over the past decade or so in some form or another, and it is something I have become particularly aware of when making several fundamental business decisions at a time. For obvious reasons, I won't go into too much detail behind the commercial sensitivities, but it would be fair to say that my delay in decision making and taking action in one particular situation had a very profound impact on several hundred colleagues with respect to their jobs and incomes. Perhaps because of the significance and difficulty of those decisions and actions, I "chose" to put them off day after day and work on other (relatively easier) tasks. Of course, I eventually got to the point where I had to take action, and at that point I did, but the regret remains. How many weeks of stress, pain, and uncertainty could I have avoided for hundreds of my colleagues had I not procrastinated?

In recent times, I have devised my own very basic technique to help me overcome procrastination. It is a mental and verbal process that I'm delighted to say works for me almost every time I feel myself falling into that situation. I call it my "starter gun call-out," and much like any race, it is based on a countdown process followed by sudden movement and ideally as fast as possible. You will recall from Olympic sprint events that every race is started with a countdown usually preceded by silence, an air of expectancy, and then the sudden flurry of arms, legs, and bodies propelled forward by the word, "GO!"

So, I devised my own and undeniably peculiar way of interrupting my brain and thought processes when the feeling of procrastination is the strongest. I say it out loud, word for word, as follows: "I have my goals, I have my purpose. On my marks, get set, GO!!!!" ...and in the split second that I say "GO," I move. I start. I commence an action—no more thinking, no more analysing. I just move. I can assure you that once I begin, even the smallest of actions is enough to kill the procrastination problem. It is my way of dealing with this challenge, and it is a phrase I've refined over the years, and it works for me. There is an excellent book I heartily recommend by Mel Robbins called *The Five Second Rule,* and it delves into how the countdown process works to interrupt the thinking process of the brain and gets you moving. She bases it on the countdown to the launch of a rocket, "five, four, three, two, one, GO!" where you simply move, get up, and take action on the word "GO."

Lastly, do not beat yourself up about procrastination. You can't undo or change the decisions or actions you may or may not have taken in the past, but you can control the choices you make the next time you face the same problem. Think about where you want to be, let's say, in six days, six weeks, six months, or even six years from now. Think about your purpose and why you have goals and systems to enable you to achieve this. Reflect on the actions required to get you there, and when taking action seems difficult, remind yourself, "I have my goals, I have my purpose, I'm on my marks, so I need to get set and GO!"

Code-byte 4D: "Investing in Your Bamboo Tree"

When I am in a coaching discussion with clients, and particularly in the first few weeks of working together on the SUCCESS Code®

methodology, I often hear, "I have been working on this goal system for weeks, and I still haven't achieved my goal". The doubts begin to surface and if we don't recognize and deal with these doubts, the critical actions required to maintain progress typically slow down and even cease. Procrastination will begin to surface its ugly head. Most frustratingly, clients, and indeed many of us in life and business, often decide to give up and walk away from future success right at the moment we're about to achieve a noticeable and significant breakthrough! There must be some universal law, such as the law of gravity or Murphy's Law, which suggests that success and achievement were within your grasp had you persisted a bit longer!

A metaphor that I use to explain the importance of continuing to invest in and maintain your actions is that of the Chinese bamboo tree. After this amazing tree is planted, you will not see anything break through the soil for many months, perhaps with the exception of a tiny shoot. However, it is vital that the soil and the tiny shoot be watered and looked after as much as possible, ideally daily. Now all you can see on the surface is this tiny shoot, and despite all the tending, feeding, and watering, nothing seems to be happening that is visible. Yet under the surface, the bamboo tree is developing a massive, fibrous root structure, spreading far and wide under the soil, invisible to the human eye. After two years or so, the Chinese bamboo tree will begin a sudden growth frenzy, reaching a possible height of 80 feet in a matter of days! This is only possible because of the strength and depth of the root systems it developed over two years.

Remember your *DART-board Goal System toolkit* and the resulting goal systems you focused upon in your "Dynamic Dozen" are an investment into several aspects of the rest of your life. For some goals, this process may result in success in just days, but many of your goals may take weeks, months, or in some instances with your huge, transformational goals, years to achieve. Maintaining your actions and working on your systems even when you cannot see the obvious external signs of achievement are crucial to your success, so understand the investment you are making and keep moving forward.

Yet another example to highlight this important point is to try and think of every action you take toward achieving any of your goals as a single grain of sand. Now imagine a set of scales with a 1-pound weight on one side and an empty tray on the other. The scales will tip firmly to the side with the 1-pound weight. If you dropped one tiny grain of sand into the empty tray on the other side, nothing would happen as the weight would still be far heavier than the grain of sand. However, if you add grain upon grain upon grain over time, the single grains of sand will eventually form a pile of sand, and there will come a time when the addition of just one more grain to the pile will be enough to tip the scales the other way. Therefore, every action you take toward your success, be it small, medium, or large, makes a difference, even if you don't see it at that particular point. Every grain of sand is the equivalent of one action, and just one action can and will generate that magical movement, the momentum, and success.

Investing in yourself may be the most profitable investment you ever make. The effort you put into consistently investing in yourself day after day plays a huge role in determining the quality of your life now and in the future, so keep taking action consistently.

Code-byte 4E: Destructive Comfort Zones

Another major reason we convince ourselves not to take action is when these actions require us to leave our comfort zone. Your "comfort zone" is that safe, warm, familiar place where you feel comfortable. Everything just seems easy in this place, so there is absolutely no reason to move out of it. It's called a comfort zone for a reason—it's comfortable, and we all like comfort.

Unfortunately, staying in your comfort zone is impossible if you truly wish to achieve your purpose, goals, and everything else in life that you desire. Leaving your comfort zone is where the magic happens. Yes, it is scary, and yes, you are stepping into the unknown at times, and it is uncomfortable, but when you do this as part of your purpose and goal systems, it is also a rewarding, exciting, and sometimes a completely addictive place to go to.

I'm sure we've all read plenty of articles and heard people talk about the importance of leaving your comfort zone. I can certainly testify about such matters when I decided to leave my corporate career behind to follow my purpose and passion to write books, speak, and coach on the SUCCESS Code® and start my own business. I had been on someone's payroll for three decades, drew a regular monthly salary, and enjoyed frequent bonuses and all the perks of a senior executive who was considered successful throughout my career. Yet I was planning to leave this and work for myself, giving up all of the certainty and security I described to work for myself. Gulp! Talk about stepping out of a comfort zone, and despite all the obvious fears and concerns, I do not have a single regret. When you step out of whatever comfort zones that are holding you back, you will see what I mean.

"Introducing Steve McNicholas." It was my first keynote speech for which I had charged the client a fee and I was incredibly nervous as the lights dimmed and the microphone kicked in. I was yet again way out of my comfort zone by charging people to hear me speak! One hour later, I returned to my seat after a wonderfully positive reaction to my speech. When I eventually got back to my seat, I just sat there for a few moments as my heart rate continued to pound, but I also felt more alive and excited about what I wanted to do for my career, that I was working to the "purpose" I knew was within me. That would not have ever happened if I'd stayed in my comfort zone.

Your comfort zone is an artificial mental boundary that gives you a sense of security and the pleasant feeling of comfort. Within this artificial zone, everything is routine, everything is familiar and safe. However, when we constantly live inside our comfort zone, we are rarely, if ever, pushed. As a result, we rarely tap into our full potential and achieve a fraction of what we're capable of. Often, people stay in a job or relationship just because of its familiarity and security and the fact that the unknown seems scary and daunting. After all, why break a routine if it's comfortable? It's this very comfort that can stifle and suffocate action.

Have you even been in a situation where the pressure was on you? It may be a presentation to a client with a big contract up for grabs, a meeting with your boss to present a new product idea to the management, a first date with someone, or a new class to learn a new subject, and it's the first time you meet your fellow students. Just when you feel like the last thing you need is anxiety or nerves, they kick in, and you start having conversations with yourself and fear the worst. "What if the client dislikes me? What if my boss thinks my idea is stupid? What if my date doesn't like me? What if nobody in the class even speaks to me?" It may feel awful, and you would be tempted to jump back into that comfort zone. But in reality, a little anxiety is a good thing because just outside of our comfort zone lies a space called *optimal anxiety*, which is a sweet spot of human performance where we are motivated to succeed. Just like an athlete who has just prepared and warmed up for a big race, jumping about nervously before getting into the starting blocks, *optimal anxiety* is the space where we are prepared to perform at our best and as shown below, it is the place just "outside" comfortable.

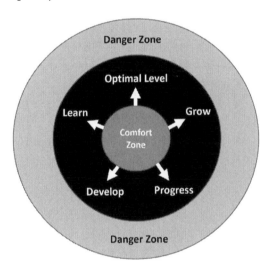

Comfort Zone Summary: Several positives when we step "outside" the zone

When we encourage and push ourselves to get out of our comfort zones, the first thing we notice is that we start feeling anxious about what we're going to do. We may not be fully aware of the anxiety manifesting itself through physical changes, but it does. This can typically include increased heart rate, clenching of muscles, more rapid breathing, perspiration, and an increased level of alertness. Anxiety is a perfectly normal human response. It is designed to keep us safe and was incredibly important in our evolution as humans. It stopped us from entering dangerous situations and prepared us to get out of them quickly if we found ourselves in one. In a dangerous situation, our "fight or flight" response is typically heightened, preparing our bodies to get ready for action through immediate increases in our stamina, alertness, and performance.

You've probably read stories of people who have performed what seemed like incredible, superhuman feats in emergency situations that evoke a very strong "fight or flight" response. This response is not something we can invoke at will. Small levels of anxiety can increase our performance levels, but if we experience too much anxiety, it can have a detrimental effect on our performance, causing it to decline, and we perform way below our normal potential. This is why stepping beyond our comfort zones and taking action and consistently pushing our boundaries a little further each time, brings us closer to achieving our optimal anxiety levels and hitting peak performance in a structured way, reducing the chances of us pushing too far. Pushing too far however, can lead to us being extremely anxious and stressed and therefore into the danger zone, where performance, growth and success is highly unlikely.

Your comfort zone isn't a bad thing, by the way—far from it. We all need a space where we can relax and feel at ease and comfortable. So, why do we need to push ourselves outside of our comfort zone from time to time? Sometimes, a goal can seem out of reach and unachievable. Because of this, we often put off chasing the dream, and we settle for mediocrity (or what is achievable within our comfort zone). But as we push ourselves outside our comfort zone into optimal anxiety, such challenges will become easier, and our comfort zone will expand. Eventually, things that previously scared us from taking action will become part of our comfort zone, and we will then seek to achieve more than we previously thought possible.

Comfort can lead to laziness, and while comfort may feel good in the short term, sacrificing productivity and not taking the action we need to take to achieve our goals will lead to regret in the long run. No matter the goal and system you have developed to help you achieve what you want, there will undoubtedly be a stage where you'll have to make a move that feels uncomfortable. There are plenty of ways to step outside your comfort zone and extend the boundaries of what you are capable of, and I have referenced a few as follows:

- **Coach yourself through new (and scary) situations.** Some good self-talk can really help you step outside your comfort zone. Simply repeat some encouraging, positive phrases to yourself, and use your name in the first person to make it more effective. You can say something like, "Steve, I know you're scared, but you're going to try this anyway. Just think about how excited you will feel when you take this action toward your goal. You can do this, so let's go!" Over the years, I have even found a quiet spot or gone to the bathroom for privacy and talked myself through a challenge that I know I have to face.

- **Think BIG but take SMALL steps.** Maybe you want to start your own business, quit your day job to chase your passion and be super successful within a year of starting! This may seem like one huge, unattainable mountain to climb, but when approached in small steps, you can slowly push the boundaries of what you feel is possible. Before you quit your job, set a goal to go and interview one business owner who is operating in the area or specialisation that you want to work in and explore his or her feedback and opinion. Taking that initial step outside of your comfort zone may seem small compared to the "mountain," but it will help you move toward your greater goal.

- **Visualize challenges as chances to grow.** The biggest obstacle keeping you from stepping out of your comfort zone is almost always fear, especially fear of failure. Instead of focusing on the possibility of failure, think of steps outside your comfort zone as opportunities. You may be right around the corner from changing your life for the better! Stepping out of your comfort zone can make you happier and more fulfilled. Keep those positive possibilities at the front of your mind to push out the fears. For example, you want to throw your name in the hat for a promotion that just came up at work, but you're terrified of being ridiculed if you do not get the job. Instead of focusing on that outcome, imagine what could happen if you got the job and visualise it happening. You often make up considerably more nonsense in your mind than what actually exists in reality.

- **Picture the worst-case scenario to put your fear in perspective.** Ask yourself, "What's the worst that could possibly happen here if I go for this and take action?" Think about ways you could deal with those circumstances if they happened. Once you're prepared for the worst (which will very rarely ever be as bad as you'll imagine!), you can only be happily and pleasantly surprised by something better! Experience over the years has taught me that the outcome is never as bad as I may have imagined it to be.

Again, there is a whole science behind this and how to overcome self-doubt and fear. This code-byte reminds you that whatever prevents your taking action is likely to be preventing you from living the life that you dream of. Nobody is suggesting this is easy. In our minds, it can even be terrifying and exciting at the same time! However, what is certain to me and what I know from experience are that when you step outside this zone, even just occasionally, the lessons, experiences, and excitement are incredible and only serve to encourage you to do it again and again! Go for it!

Summary Reflection 1

If the goals and systems you designed in Code Block 3 have any chance of succeeding, you are going to have to take action. There is no substitute for this, and sometime the required actions will need you to be brave, bold, and clear on the reasons why such actions are required. You must always understand that you have the potential to take any action, and as we saw in the Potential Loop model, once you take that first step and see those first signs of progress and results, belief grows, and the loop builds momentum. It all starts with you. Yes, there are challenges to taking action, but often they sit with you. Whether it is procrastination, a fear of the action, or the fear of being uncomfortable, all of these are 100 percent yours to overcome. You can overcome them with a few deep breaths and a chat with yourself to "just go for it." Unfortunately, and there's no other alternative here, if you do recognize these challenges in your life and in the pursuit of your goals, you are just going to have to overcome them. Plenty of ideas, support, and techniques exist to do just that (remember that success leaves clues), as well as those techniques I myself have used, so find them and apply them because your future success, achievement, and happiness depends upon you taking action.

Summary Reflection 2

Quite a while ago, I realized that those who have succeeded in whatever aspect of my life that I was focused upon improving almost always left "answers or directions or clues" on how they did so! For many years, I always had goals for several areas of my life whenever I reassessed my own *DART-board Goal System toolkit*. These included health, finances, career, personal growth, and so on, and when building the very best goal system that I could to ensure I succeeded, I only had to look for the "clues" left behind by others.

One of the best things about living in today's high-tech world is the fact that almost everything you want to do or have a goal for has already been done by somebody else, and it does not take long to understand the specific actions they took to succeed. It does not matter whether the goal is about losing weight, running a marathon, starting a business, becoming financially independent, overcoming an illness, finding a new partner, or changing jobs successfully. Someone has already done it and will have left many answers in the form of books, articles, manuals, YouTube videos, university classes, online courses, seminars, or workshops.

Take these lessons or clues as sufficient authority to support the actions you need to take. If someone has successfully completed the same goal that you have and then kindly taken the time to explain the action they took to do it, you don't really have much of a choice here, do you? You have a step-by-step guide and an assurance that following these actions has led to success and achievement. I understand that you may need to try different steps or do something different, but we know from the earlier code-bytes the importance and amazing benefits of doing so.

Summary Reflection 3

Finally, be aware of your understandable desire and expectation to immediately see tangible success for those actions you do take. Every single action, like a grain of sand or root of a bamboo tree, is making a significant difference even if it doesn't seem obvious and visible straight away. Keep investing in yourself by taking action, day in, day out, confident in the fact that you know why you are doing it, and when the bamboo shoot does break the soil, incredible growth and success will be visible in a short period of time. You have to keep inching forward, and taking action is the only way to do that.

Think about the analogy of driving a car on the highway. You often merge onto the highway from a ramp or side road of some sort. Although you might be going slower than the highway traffic at that point, you know where you are heading (your goal), and you know you need to be on this highway (the system and actions) to get to your destination. Sometimes, even though everything is going okay and you are progressing along nicely, traffic suddenly slows down for no obvious reason. You find yourself inching forward behind the car in front of you and occasionally jumping lanes when you think the traffic next to you is going quicker. You then get frustrated when the traffic in the lane you left appears to move faster than the one you moved to! However, all this time, you continue to take action to inch forward. Suddenly and for no obvious reasons, despite there being no accident or incident of note, the traffic suddenly speeds up again, and you are quickly back up to the necessary speed and progressing quickly toward your destination once again. You still have no idea why the traffic slowed, but it's moving freely now, and you are back up to speed.

At no point in the journey, however, do you just leave your car in the middle of the highway and get out, announcing that you will not be driving the car anymore! This is like the journey you need to make to achieve your goals. You have to keep taking action to inch forward. Occasionally, if it's not working, you will "change lanes" to try and make progress, and that's fine. What is critical is that you keep taking action and keep moving forward. It might take longer than expected, but you cannot get to your destination without moving forward. Never get out of the car and walk away!

*Compelling Action 4*_____

Update your *Code-Breaker Toolkit* sheet; under Code Block 4. Take a moment to reflect and enter THREE tactics, strategies or plans that you intend to take or use to ensure you take action on your goal systems and/ or overcome any potential barriers to doing so.

_____

Code Block 5
Erase Your Limiting Beliefs

"Our limitations and success will be based, most often, on our own expectations for ourselves. What the mind dwells upon the body acts upon"

– Dennis Waitley

Many of us have beliefs that limit our personal success. They may be beliefs about our own capability, what it takes to succeed, how we should relate to other people in our lives, or even common, everyday beliefs that modern science or research has long since refuted. Becoming aware of and then moving beyond your limiting beliefs is a crucial step toward becoming more successful and fulfilled in life. It is so important that it warrants its own Code Block, and it is a subject that I want you to become more aware of to be able to manage, and when necessary, overcome your limiting beliefs.

What do I mean by *limiting beliefs*? Well, they are those little voices in your mind that convince you that you can't be, do, or have something. They take the wonderful and positive ideas, goals, and dreams that you hold in your mind and within seconds quickly crush them! The best way I can describe our limiting beliefs is that they are like weeds that grow in the garden. They are rarely pretty. They tend to suffocate all the natural flowers and plants around them, and if left alone for too long, they completely take over the garden so that little to nothing can grow or flourish there. Yes, you can apply a "weed treatment" to them, and it can stop their growth for a short time, but they nearly always come back again and again. It takes constant and relentless monitoring and treatment to keep them controlled and hidden.

These "weeds" can grow in your mind, and no doubt they already do. We all have them for various reasons, but we need to spot, treat, and control them, and where possible, erase them. Just like weeds, your limiting beliefs, if left alone, can suffocate all of the progress you have made or plan to make in the time ahead of you.

Beliefs are essentially assumptions we make about ourselves, others, and how we expect things to be in our world. We have all these theories, ideas, and explanations about how things are and how they ought to be. Likewise, we make all these conclusions about life and about other people, all of which help us make better sense of the world. In other words, we use beliefs as anchors that help express our understanding of the world around us. It's important to note that beliefs are *not* facts. However deeply ingrained they may be in your mind, beliefs can be mistaken as facts. These beliefs are often nothing more than conclusions you have drawn based on your childhood experiences. Back then, these beliefs may have served a purpose, and that is why you have held onto them for so long. However, as an adult, these beliefs no longer serve a purpose. In fact, these beliefs may actually become a hindrance as they are no longer compatible with your current life or circumstances. Your life has changed; however, your beliefs have remained constant, which is why you can often feel stuck and restricted in the present.

The biggest problem, though, and why this subject has its own Code Block to help you move forward past this, is that your limiting beliefs force you to live way below your potential. The media, TV, our friends, relatives, and the people we come in contact with every single day keep feeding us limiting beliefs without our ever noticing. "Be careful!" "Watch out!" "What if it goes wrong?" "You might get hurt!" "You might get fired!" "You won't enjoy it!" "Nobody has ever done that!" "What if it fails or doesn't work?" And on they go. This Code Block and the code-bytes that follow are intended to get you to reflect on your limiting beliefs in a different way but always with the purpose of choosing to overcome them. You need to learn to recognize, minimize, and then deal with them in order to not let them prevent you from pushing on through with the goals and goal systems you have built and when you need to take specific action. Don't let them stop you.

So, where do these limiting beliefs come from? For most of us, it's typically a result of early childhood programming. Whether they knew it or not, our parents, grandparents, teachers, and other adult role models may have quite often said, "That's too much for you to handle," "You can't do that," "You'll never be that rich," "Let me do that for you as I can do it better," "Not now; maybe next year when you're bigger and stronger," "You can't do that; you might get hurt," "Don't risk it, stay safe, get down from there." I am sure there are countless more, and the constant repetition and recitation of these beliefs by those we love, admire, and respect helps limit our ability or potential us in some way. We take this sense of "inability" into adulthood where it gets further reinforced through workplace beliefs, mistakes, and other failures as we set off on the path of life: "These targets are unachievable," "That client won't buy," "You won't get promoted." There are hundreds of limiting beliefs that are formed by what gets said at work.

Considering our childhood beliefs, those that we form at work, and then what we overlay with what we see and hear on social media and in the press about "bad things happening," numerous limiting beliefs are well and truly formed! Quite sad really, but the exciting bit about all of this is that pretty much every single limiting belief you have is *unlikely* to be true! If other people have accomplished what you need to do, then so can you. If you don't have the knowledge and you think that limits you, there is someone out there who can teach you. Until you try and fail, how do you know you can't? Even if you do fail, you haven't really, as all you have done is produce a result. At the very least, you have an understanding of how to improve this result next time!

Being aware and conscious of your limiting beliefs is key. Approximately 99.9 percent of them are false. They are not true and do not reflect the potential you have to succeed, but if we don't tackle them, these weeds in our minds, then they can strangle our progress by:

- Creating false perceptions through which we see our lives playing out, and that skews our ideas and opinions of what we are truly capable of and keeps us stuck in negative life thoughts and patterns;

- Believing these thoughts and patterns mean we continue to live within their confines, further fulfilling the limiting belief and suffocating our happiness and potential even more;

- Creating a repeating cycle of self-sabotage when it comes to those areas of our life that we know we want to change.

For the first three code-bytes in this Code Block, I am going to explore and offer some reassurance about the most common areas where limiting thoughts can restrict your potential. These are lifted from the main sectors of the *DART-board Goal System toolkit* and from my own experience in hearing the same old limiting beliefs presenting themselves time and time again. In the remaining code-bytes, I will share a few specific techniques to help you manage these "weeds" and allow your dreams, goals, and aspirations to flourish.

Code-byte 5A: Limiting Beliefs in Career Progression

Today, most people spend more time at work than they do anywhere else. In the earlier parts of this book, you were asked to take some time to think about your purpose and assess how satisfied and content you were in your professional life. If you then went on and set goals in this area of your life as many do, it is important you face up to the limiting beliefs that may prevent you from succeeding to your maximum potential. How can we thrive when we spend so much time at a place where we are actively disengaged or feel like we should be aiming for something bigger? We know the answer, we have to make the changes and take the actions necessary to move toward this. But first, let's examine a few of the common beliefs you may have holding you back here.

"I could never do that" is pretty much born out of fear. The fear of failing is probably the number-one reason that holds us back from success especially in the work context. The irony of this however is that fear of failing is only ever created by ourselves. It's not real, it's a mindset or state of mind that you develop and grow, and it is rarely if ever based on anything tangible.

Ask yourself, "What is it that I am actually scared of, and what is it that I think I might 'fail' at?" The basic truth here is that there is no such thing as a "failure," there are only results. You do something and you get a result. You learn from that result, and you do it again if necessary. Fear can immobilize you from taking any action, and there's nothing I can write, teach, or coach to take that fear away for you.

However, what I do know is you can acknowledge, appreciate, and overcome this fear by reminding, talking, and informing yourself that countless others have done this. Tell yourself that you need to do this to move forward. Think of the positives—the progress and satisfaction you will have when you take this action. Understand that the fear you have is *not* reality. Think of FEAR as an acronym: **f**alse **e**xpectations **a**ppearing **r**eal! I prefer **f**ind **e**nergy **a**nd **r**ise! The big secret here is to learn how to use fear instead of letting fear use you.

"I just don't have the skills or talents to do that job." It is hard to think of any new job you start where the standard process does not involve a training or induction period, commonly referred to as on-the-job training. Considering starting your own business? There are countless programs on how to do this successfully and professionally. My point here, and the conversation you must have with yourself when these limiting beliefs begin to take hold, is that you have more skills and talents than you think you have, and there are ways to help develop your skill base. If you have a goal in life, then you also clearly have a passion for it, which is just as valuable as the skills and competencies you need to act upon it! Skills can be learned and built up, so don't allow this excuse to prevent you from moving forward.

Success in life requires progress, so keep learning, growing, pushing, and telling yourself that "if I don't do this, if I just stagnate, then I will not prosper and progress, and that is not an option here." Be the creator of your life and decide that it is going to be lived on your terms. You have the purpose. You have the goal system. You have at least some of the knowledge, skill, and talent to do this, and there are countless ways to learn more. When you commit, there will be a way.

"Those who succeed in work are just lucky, and I'm not." I am hoping that by now you know you can overcome this limiting belief by yourself. People we commonly label "successful" share a common set of qualities or personality aspects, namely focus, purpose, drive, passion, and taking action to achieve their goals. Well, so do you! This is not about luck; this is about doing what you know you need to do, what you know you can do, and most important, what you now know you must do. All it takes is one small shift in your mind-set and you can do this. Never, ever tell yourself any longer that the people who are succeeding are luckier than you. You can choose to be as successful, even more successful if you want, than 99 percent of the people on this planet, so get on and do it.

Code-byte 5B: Limiting Beliefs in Finance and Money

This is a powerful and emotive subject and something we all have opinions, beliefs, and worries about. It's just a small word, *money*, and yet it can bring feelings of guilt, joy, happiness, jealousy, anger, and when we perceive that we have enough of it, freedom and happiness.

Now, whether you have set goal systems in place from your *DART-board Goal System toolkit* to achieve goals in the finance section or not, there are still a number of common limiting beliefs here that we all have had at some point and are well worth reflecting on. In most of the modern world, the framework exists for each and every one of us to achieve the financial goals and aspirations that we seek, but a bit like the discussion of fear in the previous code-byte, we need to learn to spot and overcome those limiting beliefs about money before those weeds take over the garden. Some of the more common ones are as follows.

"Money is the root of all evil." A common belief that is often linked to the perception that those who have wealth have probably obtained it deceptively, dishonestly, or through ill means! if you haven't decided to frame this area of your life in a positive sense yet, and you still hold thoughts of money as being something bad, or even evil, then you need to change this limiting belief. It's an abstract belief and almost always comes from a view formed from "looking from the outside." Maybe you

have had some bad experiences with people perceived as wealthy and created the limiting belief that, with money, everybody will become like this. Or, maybe you think negatively about people who make money and wealth as their one and only goal in life, when they start chasing money at all costs and get blinded to other important values such as love, compassion, and helping others. All of this thinking, of course, is wrong, and it is not the fault of money.

Money was created as an exchange medium for the value of traded goods. So, it is just an expression of perceived value. Those individuals who are deemed to have a lot of money and wealth means that they have in some way, or several ways, created a lot of value over time. This could be value derived from products or services (customers who pay for the product) or for knowledge and skills (employers who pay you for your competence and talent). When you set up a goal system to achieve your financial goals, be clear that understanding how much value you are going to create for customers or worth for an employer is equally important as the financial figure you set for yourself. When the two are aligned, there is no limiting belief.

"It is just too difficult to become wealthy." You don't get wealthy by only working hard; you get wealthy by doing the right things, namely applying the successful strategies that countless others have to build wealth. One method is to look for the "smart" way to become wealthy. I don't mean in the sense of looking for a quick fix or doing questionable things, but by understanding what leads to wealth. This means understanding how you can create real and lasting value for others, and then offering it for a good price. This is true if you are a business-owner, self-employed, or employed. If you work in sales, you can often quickly understand the power of your efforts here; it is almost always rewarded by money or commission. If you run a business, you should take time to truly understand the value that your products and services provide and work hard at sharing that value with your target market in every channel you can. Our rewards in life are almost always in correlation to the level of service and value we provide in life.

Additional strategies will often include saving a set percentage every month, leveraging the power of compounding returns, and finding investment options that may have risk but provide greater returns. Once more, the methods, tools, and techniques of building wealth are freely available if you search for them. You can do it. You can increase your value, and from there, you can build wealth, and it does not take a lifetime!

"Money can't buy me happiness anyway." Perhaps because of the explosion of social media and the common knowledge available about who has got what, who earns what, who has just bought what, and so on, we tend to see money and happiness as mutually exclusive. The limiting belief here is "money can't buy me happiness," but then again, neither does poverty I suppose. Personally, my own view on this is that YES, money can buy you happiness, but only when you define *happiness* clearly for yourself. (Think back to your purpose in Code Block 2.)

I have a purpose to help as many people as I can unlock the SUCCESS Code® to success, happiness, and achievement in life and business. It is why I write, speak, and teach about the subject with passion and enjoyment. Now, if I am fortunate enough to earn money from doing this, from helping people, then happiness to me is spending time with my family and going on family vacations. Money helps with that. If I am able to hire someone to assist in household chores, not only am I happy that I have more time to spend on things I want to do but also because I am able to help another person earn and build wealth by providing the service I am paying for. Money helps me do that. I am happy dining with friends. I am happy watching my favourite sports team. I am happy when I am experiencing things I value, and money helps to do that. Materialistic possessions are nice to have (the house, the car, gadgets), and money is needed for that, but it is experiences that make you truly happy.

Code-byte 5C: Limiting Beliefs in Relationships

It is vital that I state at this point that I am not an advice columnist or some form of relationship counsellor. I guess we have all had similar limiting thoughts and beliefs when it comes to the relationships we have. Relationships are our deepest and most intimate connections, and they are a place where we can feel our most vulnerable, open, and raw but also incredible joy, happiness and intimacy. Therefore, if you have set goals and systems to improve these aspects of your life from the "DART-board" assessment, do not let the stories you tell yourself ruin or reduce your potential for incredible success and fulfilment in this hugely significant aspect of our lives.

"I cannot ask; what if they say no?" The fear of rejection in approaching anyone we may be attracted to can cripple the vast majority of individuals and often leads to intense regret and unhappiness the very moment the situation has passed. "If only I asked him." "If only I just went and spoke to her." Science has already proven that in the moment we perceive rejection, our heart rate drops, our pupils dilate, and our body typically falls into fight or flight mode. However, these physical reactions often only last for a few seconds versus the hours, days, and longer periods of regret because we did not speak up, make the first move, start the conversation, or just say hello.

The actual reality as well is that *rejection* is often just a meaning you make up. Did they REALLY reject you, or were they just unavailable? How can you possibly understand what other things are happening in that person's life at that moment that might suggest that even if right now is not a good time to develop the conversation, tomorrow might be? Also, how much better do we feel when we take a deep breath at a moment of nervousness or fear and then go for it! You approach the person you are attracted to, you speak, and whatever the outcome, you feel proud that you did it. No disasters happened. The person might have agreed to meet up with you again or might have not, but you won't have regret eating away at you. The next time this situation presents itself, you can do it. Do not put off chasing happiness and love in a relationship because you fear a no. You have no idea whatsoever what the person might say, and until you overcome this limiting belief, you are putting off progress to a huge goal you have set for yourself.

"If I start a relationship, it will probably fail like the last one." Having and holding onto memories and feelings from our past clearly help shape and form our beliefs today. That can be positive as well as negative, of course. Assuming, therefore, that any pain or upset you experienced in a past relationship is always going to materialize again in the next one, and that you should try and avoid such potential pain and heartache by remaining alone, are totally unfounded ideas. Remember that we never really fail at anything we do, we just get a result. If a past relationship ended, that was the result, so try and take a balanced view of why you got that result. What were the lessons you learned about yourself, and how would you try and do things differently when the next relationship starts?

Ruling out the chance of happiness and joy with someone else because of the pain and hurt from a previous relationship is a dangerous limiting belief. There really are no justified resentments you should hold because, quite frankly, the only person suffering and missing out on life is you! You have suffered enough. Trust in your goal and your systems to achieve what you want and go and try again, learning from the results of the past when necessary.

"I have to find X, have Y, and do this by Z." Well, talk about putting pressure on yourself and applying the most specific of limiting restrictions! Just how much more pressure do you put on yourself for something as important to you as a relationship by putting a stopwatch on the goal? Yet, for many of us, that is what we do. I know several friends who in the rush to make these self-set deadlines have formed relationships that were ultimately painful and unfulfilling but took years to come to this conclusion. I understand that it can be hard to wait to find that ideal person that checks all of your boxes, but just take the stopwatch out of it. It can save you months, often years, of frustration when you take each opportunity to form a relationship as naturally as you can.

Developing the belief "that when you are meant to find the right person you will" is a much better belief. It will help you avoid settling or pushing ahead when your instinct says not to because you hear this awful clock ticking away. Ultimately, it will keep you open to the right person for you when he or she comes along. Have faith. Have patience. And make sure your goal systems are built to keep you active in social circles, hobbies, and the like so you are always in a place where the opportunity might present itself.

These three code-bytes on career, money, and relationships all have a common theme that's true of all limiting beliefs: They exist in your own mind, but they can be recognized, understood, and then overruled. When you start to see the progress you can make and the potential you have, you will find that you can manage these beliefs positively and consistently. However, like weeds in the garden, they never disappear completely, so make sure you keep guarding against that happening.

Code-byte 5D: The Seven-Step Weed Killer!

It is pretty common in the SUCCESS Code® that by working through the first four Code Blocks, you will no doubt have already begun to identify several of your own limiting beliefs that could and will slow down your progress if unchecked. We know these are the limiting beliefs that are holding you back in life, and this is unfortunately where most people stop. They think that just having an awareness of such beliefs will now magically cause them to "think differently about their lives and circumstances" and those horrible, negative, suffocating weeds have all been destroyed, just like that!

Being aware of your beliefs will indeed encourage you to think differently about them, but it is only a start. Your limiting beliefs will have a lot of historical investment behind them, meaning you have probably held such beliefs for many years, which is where the problems lie. Whenever you have a high level of emotion invested in something, it creates a barrier to change. You will need to cut down these weeds, and this will require some hard work. In fact, the deeper the roots are, then the more work this process is going to be, but the benefits of doing so will be incredible.

So, how do we do this? Well, I have a seven-step process that you can consider. For this to benefit you, however, you need an hour in a place where you know you can sit and think and won't be disturbed. You need a pen and paper, and you need to be prepared to think, be honest, and be willing to begin to destroy these weeds in your mind that might and perhaps already do, prevent your success, achievement, and progress.

Step 1: Choose Your Desired Outcome: Your very first step is to choose your desired outcome. This will help you gain clarity about what it is you would like to change. Ask yourself:

- What goals am I truly wanting to achieve in my life, work, or career?

- What's currently preventing me from achieving these goals?

- What kind of person would I ideally like to become?

- What is it specifically about me that I would like to change?

- What specific beliefs of mine are not working for me?

- What beliefs are preventing me from achieving my desired outcomes?

Once you are clear about the limiting beliefs that are holding you back, you can move to step two of this process.

Step 2: Question Your Limiting Beliefs: Your limiting beliefs are only as strong as the references that support them. And, often your limiting beliefs probably have a plethora of references that influence your perspective on reality. It's important to keep in mind that these references were only once ideas that became opinions and later came together to form your beliefs. As such, they aren't real. They are of course real for you, but that's only your perspective. Change your perspective and opinion about them, and you will likewise throw doubt on your limiting beliefs. And that is precisely what you're going to do right now. You are going to throw doubt upon these beliefs from all possible angles.

Here are some questions to get you started on this process. This list will hopefully get you going, but you should certainly add your own questions as you move through this process. Throw doubt on your limiting belief by asking yourself:

- Is this belief really that accurate?

- Have I always believed this, and why?

- Was there a time when I didn't believe this?

- Are there times in some situations when this belief just doesn't make any rational sense?

- What evidence is there that proves this limiting belief is just non-sense?

- What's funny or strange or embarrassing about this belief?

- Is this belief helping me get what I want most in life, and will it help me reach my goals?

- What famous quotes throw doubt upon this limiting belief?

- What are the critical flaws in believing what I believe? How is it silly to even think this way?

Some of these questions might seem silly and strange. However, they are designed to help you widen your reality and perspective and the possibilities of your situation. These questions are designed to encourage you to think outside the box. They are designed to make you feel a little uncomfortable, and they are, of course, designed to help shift how you think about your limiting beliefs. The more effort you put into answering these questions, the more doubt you will throw on your limiting beliefs, and the faster you will move through this weed-killing process.

Step 3: Consider the Consequences of Your Limiting Beliefs: Having thrown doubt on your limiting beliefs, it's now time to consider the consequences of holding onto them. Really think good, long, and hard about the following questions:

- What will the consequences be if I'm unable to eliminate this limiting belief?

- How will not changing affect me physically? Emotionally? Spiritually? Financially?

- How will not changing or tackling these weeds affect my life?

- What are the short-term consequences of not changing?

- What are the potential long-term consequences of not making this change?

- How will fixing this issue make me feel?

- Given all this, why is it important to make this change right now?

The more pain you associate with holding onto this belief, the more motivation you will have to make a positive change in your life. For this reason, it's paramount that you move through these questions progressively one at a time and fully acknowledge and appreciate the pain, anger, and frustration passing through you when you consider the implications. Feel the anger, experience the grief, think about the regrets, and even allow yourself to get emotional and angry. The more anger, annoyance, and frustration you generate, the more motivation you will have to change.

Step 4: Choose a New Empowering Belief to Adopt: You must now choose a new empowering belief that you would like to use moving forward. The one guiding principle that you must follow here is to make sure that this new belief is believable. If it's not believable, then you will, unfortunately, fail to condition it into your psyche. To unlock this new empowering belief, take into consideration the goal that you want to achieve, the person that you want to become, and the core values you want to uphold, then ask yourself the following set of questions from a third-person perspective:

- What would this person likely believe while in pursuit of this goal?

- What would this person believe about him- or herself?

- What would this person believe about his or her goal?

- What's this person's attitude like? How does this person think about this goal?

- What would this person believe after having achieved the goal?

- How would this person think about the obstacles confronted along the journey?

- What would this person believe if he or she had to achieve this goal again for a second time?

- What are the benefits to this person of using this new belief?

- How will this new belief help this person to attain his or her goals?

- How will this belief change the person's life for the better?

- How will this belief help this person in the short term and in the long term?

- How will all this make this person feel about him- or herself?

Why is all this important and what does all this really mean? The more reasons you can find, the more motivation you will have to change your old patterns of behaviour and replace them with these new empowering belief systems.

Step 5: Strengthen Your New Empowering Belief: Now let's look at ways you can potentially strengthen these new positive, empowering beliefs. Strengthening a belief requires taking into consideration new ways that you could build upon the references that support this new belief. Ask yourself the following:

- What kinds of behaviours, decisions, and actions could help me strengthen this belief?

- What habits or routines could help me strengthen this belief?

- What famous quotes could I find to help me strengthen this belief?

- Could I create a slogan for myself that might help me strengthen this belief?

- Are there any stories that support the message behind this new empowering belief?

- Are there any role models I could turn to that could help me strengthen this belief?

There are many ideas here that can help you strengthen your new belief. One of the most practical ideas is simply finding a handful of quotes that support the philosophy behind your new empowering belief. Write these quotes down on a piece of paper and keep them in your pocket, wallet, purse, or notebook at work. Then, whenever you feel yourself starting to fall back toward your old limiting belief, take some time to read over these quotes. This will help you get back on track. It's easy to do and what's more, each time you read these quotes, you build stronger references that will help support your new empowering belief moving forward. Likewise, keep an eye out for stories, documentaries, and films that support the thinking behind your empowering belief. Keep them listed on that sheet of paper as well, then turn to these stories for some added insight, direction, and inspiration.

Working through the belief transformation process comes down to building solid references that help support your new empowering belief. The more references you are able to collect, the stronger your new belief will become, and this will subsequently weaken your old limiting belief. Just keep building the evidence against your limiting belief and in favour of your empowering belief. Once the evidence begins to overwhelmingly support your empowering belief, that is when the tables will turn, and your mind-set will permanently shift.

Step 6: Make a Firm Decision about What to Change: You must now make a firm decision that you will begin making the necessary changes to overcome your limiting belief. For this to happen, you must have the necessary commitment, self-confidence, and motivation to make the required changes stick. Ask yourself:

- What's my commitment level to making this change?

- Do I feel confident that I can successfully make this change?

- How motivated am I to make this change?

Go through each of these questions and rank them from 1 to 10. If you're not at least at an 8 out of 10 on all three questions, then go back to the previous steps and work through them again. Don't move on unless you have reached an 8 or above. Otherwise, you're just risking your progress and your time, and when the pressure gets tough, you will continue to sabotage yourself, and the weeds will begin to grow and take over again.

Step 7: Progressively Condition Your New Belief: Having committed yourself to this new empowering belief, it's now time to progressively condition this new belief into your nervous system. And there are a few ways you can do this, but the best way I have found is just through a regular five- or ten-minute visualization session per day. (We will reference this again in the next Code Block when reviewing ways to solidify your progress each day.)

Just spend time daily visualizing yourself in your imagination, using this new way of thinking in your day-to-day undertakings. Take note of the actions you take, the decisions you make, how you talk to yourself, how you speak to others, and so on. Think about your new attitude and the results that this new belief is helping you to manifest in your life. You are in essence imagining a new and better you in your mind's eye, and then transferring the new you from your imagination into the physical world. Everything first begins in your imagination and then gets transferred across into the real world. Doing things this way will help you to develop the self-confidence you need to work with this new belief.

In the end, what's most important is reminding yourself about the value of this new belief and how it will help improve your life moving forward.

Code-byte 5E: Five Positive Affirmations before and after Sleep

I started this whole Code Block off with the analogy that your limiting beliefs are like weeds growing in the garden of your mind. If left untreated, we know the damage that weeds can do to a garden. One of the best ways to treat those weeds, therefore, is applying the treatment in advance. There is a lot of science to back up the fact that what you feed your mind throughout the day, but especially just before going to sleep and waking from sleep, has a powerful impact on your subconscious mind and can be extremely powerful in helping you when faced with limiting beliefs as you advance toward your goals. Affirmations is the technique to help here.

An *affirmation* is usually a sentence or phrase that you repeat regularly to make a formal declaration to yourself about your intention for it to become the truth. While some may say it is akin to "faking it until you make it," I see it a bit more like repeating an image or action of what I know can be true. We all have in our brains a thing called the *reticular activating system* (RAS), which is basically a filter that lets in information that we need and filters out information that we don't. If we didn't have this system, we would be bombarded with so much information that our senses would always be overloaded, and we would spend all our waking hours in a massively overwhelmed state. Instead, our brain registers what matters to us based on our goals, needs, interests, and desires.

When you say an affirmation over and over again, a couple of things happen. One is that it sends a very clear message to your RAS that this is important to you. When you do that, it gets busy on your behalf, noticing ways to help you achieve your affirmation. The affirmation is similar often to your goals. If becoming an ideal weight is the emphasis of a repetitive affirmation, you will suddenly begin to notice every gym and weight-loss product out there. If money is your affirmation theme, investment and income-earning opportunities will move to the forefront of your awareness. In essence, the affirmation can kick your creativity into high gear. Saying these affirmations at moments when your RAS is most receptive, namely as you drift off to or wake from sleep, has been shown to be the most effective way to help program the outcomes you are desiring.

So, what makes an effective affirmation? First, determine what kind of transformation you want to bring about in yourself. Is it a change in belief, a specific goal, or a clear intention? Determine what quality, attitude, value, or characteristic you want to remind yourself of or develop in yourself. Finally, if it works for you, add an emotion to the mix or a word that adds context and outcome to the statement. I personally like affirmations that feel like they come from the heart and help me toward my purpose. It is obviously important they are said in the positive rather than the negative. For example, "I am healthy and fit to achieve my goals" rather than "I am no longer fat!"

Some say it takes twenty-one days of repetition for an affirmation to form a basis in your mind, so aim to keep your affirmation going for at least a month and a habit will form. My recommendation is to try and find just a few minutes before sleep and when you wake up to practice your affirmations before showering and breakfast and the usual bombardment of daily activities kicks in.

In the beginning, you will have to consciously choose to repeat your affirmations, and it helps to have them written down close at hand. If you repeat them at every opportunity, they will begin to replace the negative mind chatter that takes over when we are not monitoring our thoughts. Here are several examples of affirmations I have found helpful over the years, some of which I still use today:

- I know I have the ability to accomplish any task I set my mind to with comfort and ease.

- I feel passionately about my life, my purpose, and my goals, and this passion fills me with excitement and energy every day.

- I can accomplish anything I put my mind to because I know the answers to all my challenges already exist; I must just go and find them.

- I have access to everything I need to overcome this challenge.

- I am excited about breaking old, negative habits and replacing them with new, positive, and successful ones.

- My time is the most valuable resource I possess; therefore, I will spend it wisely and where I know I want to spend it.

- I have the power, right now, to decide what I want to do, how I want to think, and the choices I need to make to bring my goals and dreams to fruition.

I am pretty sure you can develop your own affirmations to meet the requirements of your specific challenges but do consider this code-byte. When you decide to read and recite these affirmations as often as you can each day, see them in your mind while you say them.

Summary Reflection 1

This entire Code Block is designed to help you overcome the limiting thoughts you have in your mind regarding your ability to succeed. These limiting beliefs can do significant damage to your goals, dreams, and plans for happiness and achievement, and you cannot let them take over like weeds in the garden. Remember that they are only ever thoughts, rarely facts, so find your way to deal with them and move past them. Such beliefs will rarely ever completely disappear, and that is okay. You just need to ensure that the actions you need to take are taken, and defeating or overcoming each limiting belief, one at a time, is all that is needed to keep progressing. Find a way. Your progress through the SUCCESS Code® and to happiness, growth and achievement is far too important not to.

Summary Reflection 2

The seven-step, weed-killer process I explained earlier is a proven framework to help you with any limiting belief. Identify it. Challenge and disprove it. Build a nonlimiting, positive belief and embed it in whatever way works for you. *Affirmations* are an excellent way to embed positive, uplifting, and nonlimiting beliefs, and finding a way to do this at every possible moment in your day, especially as the last thing before sleeping and the first thing early each morning, is an excellent process to keep building confidence and beliefs to enable you to move past negativity.

Summary Reflection 3

Finally, when a limiting belief also extends into a personal weak spot or a key challenge that you have to manage yourself with (i.e. poor time management, too much procrastination, finding excuses too quickly, etc.), you typically have these four choices to address them:

1. Deny they exist and therefore fool yourself into believing that you don't have an issue!

2. Accept them and then work to turn them into strengths.

3. Accept them and find better ways to minimize their impact.

4. Alter the goal or system objective to make the weak spot irrelevant.

Always look to option 2 as the preferred way to tackle the issue. "Success leaves clues" as I mentioned earlier, and there are lots of tools, techniques, tips, and maybe even apps for your phone that allow you to progress. Your achievement, happiness, and success has got to be worth it. Do find a way to help yourself improve or address the weak spot. Investment here will pay incredible dividends.

Compelling Action 5

Update your *Code-Breaker* toolkit sheet under Code Block 5. Please enter three positive affirmations unique to you that will help you overcome any limiting beliefs you may be holding in pursuit of your goals and systems. You must read and say these affirmations aloud as often as you can each day, but especially at the start and end of each day!

Code Block 6

Solidify Your Progress Daily

"Waiting for perfect is never as smart as making progress."

– Seth Godin

People excitedly make their New Year resolutions every year, which are usually about diet, health, career change, or similar significant commitments, but there's plenty of evidence to show that over 60 percent usually give up on these goals before the end of January! A further 20 percent or more quit by the middle of February. Why do millions of people do this every year? The reason (or purpose?) behind making a resolution is often a strong one, but before we even get to Easter, only three months after the start of the New Year, the "failure to continue" rate is well over 90 percent.

The purpose of this Code Block is to ensure that you have enough tools, techniques, and ideas so that you do not fail in your journey toward the goals and dreams you have chosen for yourself at the beginning of this process. You already have a HUGE advantage over those who fail on keeping New Year resolutions. You have taken full ownership of your actions, choices, and decisions, and you understand the power of this "ownership." You have a real clarity of purpose, you understand your passions in life, and from the *DART-board Goal System toolkit*, you have defined your "Dynamic Dozen Goals" and the support systems they need. Finally, you understand the critical need for action, and you are ready to deal with those limiting beliefs and thoughts *when*, not *if*, they enter your mind.

You are already significantly equipped for success, so this Code Block is about how to maintain and regularly refresh your desire and determination to keep on progressing day in, day out. This is your daily or weekly validation (your ongoing "check-up from the neck up"). This is about finding a set of tools and techniques that are designed to keep your body, mind, and spirit focused on the right things every day as you progress toward achieving the goals you want and deserve.

I'm going to suggest a number of code-bytes that I or those I have worked with have found to be helpful and of great benefit over time. There are considerably more than five out there, but the ones I have described have definitely helped me, are used by several thought leaders in success and achievement as well as a number of clients, who have found real benefit in applying one or more of what follows. I would stress that you find at least one, or preferably more than one, that you feel will work for you. Once you find the tools that work for you, then you will form a set of powerful habits and disciplines that will positively support you for the rest of your life! As you will shortly see, some of them involve mental techniques, some of them are involve physical activity, and some are a little bit of both.

One final point about time before I go through the code-bytes. I mentioned time quite a bit in the introductory chapters. It is the most important currency that you will ever own, and while we cannot ever change or get back the time we spent in the past, we have complete control over the time we are going to spend today and tomorrow, until, of course, time runs out as it will for all of us someday. Therefore, when you are building up your plans to keep consolidating and progressing, you will inevitably have to deal with time conflicts in your schedule.

Some of the tools, techniques, or processes that I suggest will require you to find thirty minutes of time every morning or one hour every evening, for example. You may feel that you are busy enough every morning, and you have plenty to do in the evening, so there's conflict. Often, and it's understandable, you will tell yourself that you cannot fit that plan into your schedule, so you don't do it. That's when you need to make the right choice. You need to look at priorities.

You may just need to get up a little earlier or spend less time on social media or watching TV at night, preferably both. Whatever it takes, and I have tried to suggest tools and techniques that do not take a long time and can often be done less frequently than every day, but I want you to be cognizant of this challenge. You have made incredible progress and huge decisions about how you are changing your life and pursuing the dreams and goals you have identified. Do not allow this progress to be eroded by not maintaining the positive thinking, goal-system actions, and nonlimiting mind-set that got you to this point.

Code-byte 6A: Mindfulness to Focus

Mindfulness is one of the most powerful techniques for helping with the stresses of our hectic lives and for focusing with clarity on the most important things in our lives. Mindfulness also has proven, wider benefits for our all-round general well-being. To be clear, I'm not talking about hours of deep meditation and trance-like chanting in a robe, although that would be good! No, I am simply talking about setting aside maybe ten or fifteen minutes every day, ideally the first thing every morning, in a quiet, undisturbed space where you can be relaxed, rested, and mindful.

There are lots of mindfulness applications available on your phone or tablet that can help you. I just happen to use an application called Head Space and have done so for a few years now. It provides me a simple, short, ten-minute daily opportunity to let my mind clear and rest. But let's understand why even a short burst of meditation, ideally every day, is such an important tool in helping you maintain and build on your progress in unlocking the SUCCESS Code®.

To me, I find the benefits of a daily mindfulness session quite incredible. For several minutes, I am alone with one or perhaps no thoughts in my head. In our busy, frantic lives, we are bombarded with thousands of thoughts a day to process, and nothing ever really gets the attention that it deserves. Using this application, invariably in the early morning before I have turned on my laptop, phone, and similar devices, I find ten minutes to pop on my headphones, find a warm, quiet space, and be mindful. Some days it's easy and some days it's difficult to empty my mind of the worries, concerns, and plans for the day, but with practice, it becomes easier.

Usually, when meditating and after following some breathing exercises to calm down my heart rate accordingly, I find my thoughts eventually drift to my purpose. I typically find that I develop positive feelings, thoughts of gratitude, and a reassurance that I can do this. I can live to my purpose, and I will enjoy the incredible satisfaction of serving others and helping myself at the same time. I might then have a few minutes when I think about absolutely nothing, and the sense of peace and fulfilment that results from this is incredible.

There are countless books and tools to help you with mindfulness. I could not possibly summarise the benefits and techniques of this practice in this single code-byte but I would strongly recommend you to investigate what might work for you. In summary, even though I only spend ten minutes a day via a mobile phone application and some regular time in my schedule every morning, I find myself motivated, clear on my purpose and actions for the day ahead, and with a mind-set that seems fully focused on the positives in my life. Look to find a way to ensure the same for yourself.

Frequency: Ideally daily and mornings.

Time: Whatever you can, but ten minutes is more than sufficient to begin with.

Code-byte 6B: Priming for the Day

I found this particular technique when completing a development program with a guy called Tony Robbins several years ago. Tony has been at the forefront of personal development and thinking in the United States and pretty much around the globe for many years now. I have participated in a number of his programs, and one of the techniques that I continue to use to this day is what Tony describes as "priming." *Priming* is the act of taking time to adjust your thoughts and emotions so you can live your day in a peak state of positivity and optimism that you will succeed, win, and get the things done today that you need to get done.

Priming doesn't have to be a long process. It typically takes just ten minutes out of your day, again ideally in the morning. It can help you get into a peak state and change your thoughts and actions for the better. Here's how you can start priming today:

1. **Sit:** Find a chair in a relatively quiet area and sit reasonably upright. Place both feet on the floor, shift your shoulders back, chest up, stretch your neck out long, and hold your head high.

2. **Breathe:** By changing your breathing, you change your state of being. A good way to do this is to take a deep breath in through you nose, inhaling for a full six seconds, holding it for six seconds, then exhaling fully for six seconds. Try and repeat this process four, five or maybe six times with a short pause in between each set. 1 MINUTE

3. **Begin heart breathing:** Then put your hands on your heart. Feel its power and strength as you develop a calm, steady breathing pattern. 30 SECONDS

4. **Practice gratitude:** Think of three things you're really grateful for right now. They can be from your past, your present, or your future. When you think of the first thing, create as clear an image of that moment as possible, stepping into it with your mind. Really explore why you are so grateful for the situation or thing you are thinking about. After about a minute, go to the next thing, then the next. Even on bad days, you can always find something small and meaningful to be grateful for. 3 MINUTES

5. **Visualize:** Now comes the part that's like a blessing or a prayer. It can be as spiritual as you want it to be. It's nothing to do with what faith or religion you follow, if any, but more an acknowledgment that your spirit, the universe, an energy, fate, or whatever you choose to believe, is ready to help you achieve your goals. Just try to imagine a warm light coming down from above you and filling your entire body with a positive, uplifting glow and warmth. Imagine every problem in your life is being solved. Imagine that you are getting stronger, healthier, fitter, happier, more successful and so on. Ask for the best parts of you to be strengthened even more. 90 SECONDS

6. **Share:** Send all of the energy you've gotten through your visualization out to the people you love. Feel the energy going up and down, pouring out to your family, loved ones, colleagues, and friends. 90 SECONDS

7. **Focus and celebrate:** Think about the three outcomes or goals that you want the most in your life right now. You may well have more, but these are the three things that will excite you the most once they're complete. Now, think about how you would feel once they're done. Celebrate that feeling of completion and victory, visualize how it will impact those around you. As with gratitude, go through each outcome one by one, fully experiencing the feeling of success. 3 MINUTES

8. **Get ready to rock:** Now give your body a little stretch and go tackle the world!

I know that this sounds a little bit out there compared to the other ways you might have considered, but it is an incredibly powerful technique in priming you for a brilliant, positive day every morning. There are numerous videos of Tony teaching this technique on YouTube. They are well worth watching if you think this could be one of the ways you will try to consolidate your progress.

FREQUENCY: Ideally daily and mornings.

TIME: Ten minutes is the suggested amount of time.

Code-byte 6C: The 5-4-3-2-1 Mind-set

In a similar theme to code-byte 6A, which focused upon mindfulness, this one has a similar feel to it in that it's about ten minutes in duration and requires some place quiet and peaceful where you can be undisturbed. I have, however, done this technique on planes, trains, and in traffic jams, so it is something you can confidently build into your schedule every day and the reason why it is included in this Code Block. It works! The obvious difference to the mindfulness technique explained earlier is that, in this instance, we focus our thoughts on five very specific things and in a very specific order.

Once again, finding some time to be chilled, relaxed, and able to concentrate undisturbed for some ten minutes is the prerequisite. Sitting relaxed and after a few deep breaths in and out, start to focus your mind and thoughts on the following aspects of your life:

- **Five:** We start the process by reflecting on the past twenty-four hours or so and thinking and reflecting quietly on **five positives from yesterday**, five things—events, moments, or situations— that you reflect back on and feel positive about. This is different from gratitude, that comes next, but this is just trying to remind yourself of five moments that you would call positive. Maybe you caught the train when you expected to miss it; your colleague kept the elevator door open and smiled; you shared a laugh with a friend over coffee. Just let your mind wander and try and capture those five moments in the past day that impacted you positively. The more you practice this technique, the easier it becomes to recollect these positive moments.

- **Four:** With your eyes still closed and in a relaxed state, think about **four things in your life that you are grateful for**. This can be anything and everything that gives you a sense of gratitude for what you already have in your life today. For example, you could be grateful for the fact that your heart continues to beat every day, the smile from your child, the beauty of the sky, a hug from a loved one, the meal you ate yesterday, the fun and laughter you have with friends. Simply think of just four things that you are grateful for and feel that gratitude in your heart.

- **Three:** Now we move to step three, and this is about positive thoughts of the day ahead. Once again, with eyes still closed and with a feeling of warmth and happiness from your gratitude reflections, think about your day ahead. What are the **three things you wish for and expect to go well today?** This could be an important meeting at work, an exercise class at the gym today, an important conversation with a loved one, or progressing toward your goals by completing the necessary actions. Think of three things that you want to go well today, and in your mind, picture that happening. See the meeting going well, see yourself contributing, being positive, and everybody in the meeting looking at you approvingly. Even if you have to have a difficult phone call with a loved one today, imagine a positive call where you both discuss the issue, and you end the conversation feeling relieved and happy with the outcome. The point here is that instead of setting expectations for a worst-case scenario for your day ahead, you are setting expectations with and programming your subconscious mind for a positive, happy, and productive one.

- **Two:** Now, move on to thinking about **two things that you love about yourself**. Do not be shy here; there is nobody else in your mind listening to you, so tell yourself what you like and enjoy about yourself. What are your best qualities, competencies, or skills that you love most about you? Is it your sense of fun, work ethic, or your patience and kindness? Whatever you feel that you love most about you, remind yourself of these for a moment. We are constantly bombarded with information, opinions, and feedback from all channels that can make us feel inadequate or not as good as everyone else. It is essential, therefore, that this become part of your daily mindfulness session so you can program your mind with a reminder of your strengths, qualities, and the gifts you bring to others in the world by just being you.

- **One:** The final step is to just spend around **one minute thinking about your purpose and your goals**. Remind yourself why you are on this journey and why you deserve success, happiness, and fulfilment. Remind yourself that you know you will face challenges and obstacles, but you are ready for them and you know you will overcome them because the price you need to pay is worth it.

I try to practice this process every day, and it is usually not that difficult to do, and I always feel a warm glow and sense of positive expectations of a good day ahead. I'm reminded of the positives that happened to me yesterday as well as what I am already grateful for in my life and why I am pushing on toward my goals.

FREQUENCY: Ideally, every day and in the mornings.

TIME: Whatever you can spare, but ten minutes is more than sufficient to work though the five steps.

Code-byte 6D: Vision Boards

I may have mentioned this particular tool earlier in the book, but in this code-byte, I further explain them and discuss why they are very worthy of consideration in how you will choose to consolidate your progress each day. A *vision board* is a tool used to help clarify, concentrate, and maintain focus on one or a set of your specific goals. Literally, a *vision board* is any sort of board or card upon which you display images and words that represent whatever you want to be, do, and have in your life. Simply put, we humans are very busy people, and we are constantly bombarded by distractions in every moment of our waking days. Creating and using vision boards serves a number of purposes; for example, they are constant reminders of your purpose and goals and gives them clarity. They help to reinforce your daily affirmations and can keep your attention on your intentions!

I use a card system myself, that contains a mixture of images and words to help me see, feel, and be reminded of my goals and purpose as often as I get the time to study them. I certainly look at my vision board daily and carry around my notebooks and journals. I have seen wonderful examples of powerful, inspirational vision boards of poster-sized proportions and recently have noticed several such boards as screen savers on laptops! Wherever and however you can remind yourself daily by images and "seeing" your goals, the vision board can help consolidate your progress and support your understanding of why you should keep on progressing.

Another key factor to consider for creating your own vision board is that it will help you stay focused. It isn't difficult to start each day with a positive attitude, and if you are like most people, that wave of positivity will last only until you have to get out of bed! How quickly that super-positive, focused attitude can easily sink back into oblivion once you remember the tasks and challenges ahead of you in everyday life. How can you possibly remain focused on your goals while people and circumstances constantly pull you in dozens of directions at once? By using a vision board, of course!

No matter what happens during your day, your vision board is a constant reminder of where you intend to be. Appealing to you on both conscious and subconscious levels, a vision board can work wonders toward keeping your mind focused on your goal, your attention on your intentions, and your life headed in the direction you choose. By adding a visualization practice to your daily routine, you will naturally become even more focused on achieving your goals and how successful your systems are. You'll start to notice that you are more aware of the actions you need to take throughout the day to progress toward what is on your vision board, and remember, it's yours. It is personal to you; it contains the images and goals you are working toward as well as the affirmations or words that matter to you. It is a powerful tool, and when combined or incorporated into your mindfulness or 5-4-3-2-1 technique, really does help consolidate and maintain your progress toward success.

FREQUENCY: Ideally, every day and several times per day if easily visible.

TIME: Approximately 20–30 minutes to create and perhaps a few minutes of reflection time each time you review your board.

Code-byte 6E: Dump the Toxic Tellers

This particular one might scare and disturb you somewhat, but hopefully you will understand why I included it as a consideration for you in this Code Block. As a child, your parents would often tell you to "keep away from those bad kids." They believed that if you started to hang out with those kids, you would end up behaving as they did and getting into the trouble that they did. Perhaps our parents might have exaggerated the implications a little for effect, but the principle *is* true. You tend to become like the people you spend most of your time with, and that's the key lesson in this code-byte.

You have set off on an incredible journey to achieve the goals, dreams, and aspirations that you deserve and that you know and feel you should be looking to attain. Good for you, and *my* purpose in life is to help inspire, support, and show you how to do exactly that. So, that takes care of you and me, but what about everyone you spend time with in your life? This is why I suggested that you might find this task scary and disturbing.

Who are the people in your life, personally, socially, or professionally, who will *always* TELL you how bad things are? Who always seems to be moaning and complaining and blaming others for his or her situation? Who judges, criticizes, and finds negatives in everything? Are there people in your life who, simply by phoning you, bring stress, tension, and disorder? Who are the dream stealers who will tell you that your dreams and goals are impossible and look to persuade you to stop and come back to their miserable level? I think you understand the next action here: STOP SPENDING TIME WITH THESE PEOPLE!

Until you reach a point in your self-development where you can easily dismiss such negativity from these people, you should try to avoid or minimize the time you spend with them at any cost. This journey is difficult enough without such toxic input, and you are probably better off spending time alone with your own thoughts than being constantly subjected to the negative thoughts of negative people.

Clearly, the opposite to this also applies, and when you have friends, colleagues, and family members who are positive, who will support and help you in your goals and purpose for life, then go and spend time with them as much as you can! They won't steal your dreams; they will support them and help you chase bigger ones. They believe in you and want you to achieve. These are the people you must surround yourself with at any price.

FREQUENCY: As often as you recognize the issue.

TIME: No time like the present!

Summary Reflection 1

Even the finest motor vehicles ever built—think Aston Martin, Rolls-Royce, Ferrari, and the like— need regular and specific servicing to keep them tuned and performing to the maximum of their design and engine capabilities. Put the wrong quality of fuel in, add a poor-quality component, allow the wheels to become worn, and quite quickly it will be noticeable to the driver that such incredible machines, designed to perform to very high standards compared to other motor vehicles, will start to deteriorate and lose their advantage. The same principle applies here to you. In the earlier Code Blocks, you set yourself up for incredible success and achievement. It is therefore vital that you find the right "tuning" tools to keep your performance strong and your progress maintained. Look, explore, or find your own tools and processes you can build into your routines, but ensure that you are consolidating your progress often.

Summary Reflection 2

Repetition is the mother of success. Repeating a positive process over and over will form habits, and these habits can propel you forward at incredible levels. Once you have settled on the one, two, or more tools or techniques to support your progress, do not compromise. Get them in your schedule and do them every day as planned. Once they have formed the habits you seek, you will find that you never have a priority conflict. Everything else can wait until you have invested in you.

Summary Reflection 3

In code-byte 6E, I recommend spending less time with those who restrict you, drag you down, and whom I have labelled "dream stealers" and toxic! The opposite is true, of course, in that spending more time with people who are positive, excited about life, and also want to progress, grow, and achieve is a wonderful thing.

As I highlighted earlier, "success leaves clues," so why not take advantage of the ideas, experience, and proven wisdom of those who have succeeded? Why not identify one, two, maybe three mentors whom you turn to when you need advice and guidance at those critical moments in your life and in pursuit of your goals? All you have to do is ask! I know you might feel daunted and a bit apprehensive in doing so, but once more I ask you: What is the worst that could happen? They may say that they cannot help you at the moment because of time pressures, but then again, they may say, "Yes, of course I will help." So take a few minutes and make a list of those people, colleagues, and experts who you feel could help you as mentors. You may need to read up on and research individuals whom you may never have met before but have admired their success in a field you are looking to progress or achieve goals in. Once again, the task is simply to ask.

Mentors will always look to help and advise you free of charge. They want to support you, and such help is priceless. You may also consider a personal coach with specific skills and experiences whom you are prepared to pay to help you overcome any issues, challenges, or specific concerns. A coach, the right coach, will be of tremendous personal benefit to you and can be highly skilled in helping you stay laser focused on your dreams, goals, and purpose. A coach can hold you accountable for action plans and systems and keep you focussed on your top priorities, and at the same time, keep you aware of the latest news, developments, and thinking in your chosen field, and help keep you guided on the right path to success. I have used coaches for the past decade in several areas of my life and never regretted a single penny of such an investment. Something to think about!

Compelling Action 6

Update your *Code-Breaker Toolkit* sheet under Code Block 6. Please enter two of the tools, techniques, and processes that you intend to use to ensure you consolidate your progress toward your goals and success. Whatever your commit to, ensure you build time in your schedule (block it out!) to apply these tools and strategies and seek to build discipline and habit in doing them.

Code Block 7
Survey Your Achievements (and Go Again!)

"Continuous improvement is better than delayed perfection."

– Mark Twain

And finally, we come to the last Block of the Code, and if you have worked through the previous six Code Blocks and used the tools and resources to assist you, well done! You have everything you could possibly need to build and achieve the goals you have decided you want to push toward, and I have no doubt at all that you can do it.

It won't be smooth sailing. It will be tough at times but think of it like climbing a mountain. When you arrive at the foot of a mountain, it's always a bit bigger than it looked in the pictures! When you start to climb a mountain, it's always harder and more painful than you thought it would be! When the winds and changing temperatures kick in during the climb, it's always colder and scarier than you thought it would be, and at times, you have to just keep hanging on! To climb a mountain, you need help, advice, and tools to get you up there, and you will have all you need once you start. Therefore, when you get to the summit, and you will, the views, the exhilaration, and the satisfaction you feel from reaching the top of *your* mountain are so much better than you ever thought they would be! Your second thought, after the personal pride and satisfaction in succeeding, is often "bring on the next mountain, and the one after that!"

However, in this final Code Block, we need to build in the checks and balances to ensure that you remain as focused and as set up for success as you have been through the early stages of this book. We review your first walkthrough of the SUCCESS Code® and we take on board any learnings, adjust any misunderstandings, and refine our code-bytes, tactics, and process to ensure that we remain clear and focused on all the key essentials from the previous six Code Blocks.

In this final part, I have decided not to list specific code-bytes as in the previous chapters. Rather, I have outlined seven core themes from across this book that I want you to use as a "mental checklist." These core themes are the most common areas where most of us need a refresher or reminder of the core purpose behind them. Irrespective of the progress you have made getting to this point—and I am so pleased that you have—you should return to this final Code Block maybe once a month and quickly review your progress against the following seven reflections. If you sense or notice that your progress, momentum or commitment levels are reducing, go back to the specific part of the SUCCESS Code® in question and rebuild that understanding and focus. Keep refining and reviewing as you repeat the key Code Blocks over and over to achieve your "Deliberate Dozen" goals.

Review Point 1: Using the *Code-Breaker Toolkit*

At the very beginning of the book, I urged you to download this vital toolkit, or work sheet, to use as you work through each Block of the Code within the book. In every Code Block, when it came to the "Compelling Action" at the end of each chapter, you were required to reflect and make entries in this *Code-Breaker Toolkit*. This builds up into your own personal summary to keep in your wallet, purse, journal, or diary and should be small enough to be accessible to review quickly and easily. The core fundamental actions and commitments you have made to your success are captured here, so please keep your *Code-Breaker Toolkit* updated and make sure to review it often. You can always download and start a fresh toolkit as often as you need from www.unlockthecode.co.uk, and you will find it in the "Resources" section on the site.

Why is this such an important and fundamental review point? Well, considering the mountain analogy I began this Code Block with, your *Code-Breaker Toolkit* is almost like your map up the mountain. It should contain all the key information points that you need to navigate through the climb to the top. There will be many times on this journey when you will be unsure whether to turn left or right or whether to move up or across. Constant referencing your *Code-Breaker Toolkit* will help remind you of the WHY and the HOW, and that's why it's so important.

So, here are the key questions to review and rate your progress against. Where necessary, make sure you take the time necessary to reset your understanding, actions or systems.

- Is my *Code-Breaker Toolkit* fully completed and reflective of how I am thinking and feeling at this time regarding my commitment to my success?

- Have I made a clear and clarifying statement to best describe my passion and purpose for my life, and do I still feel this statement is true, accurate, and representative of my thoughts and feelings?

- Do I find time at least once per week, more often if possible, to take a few minutes and read through the *Code-Breaker Toolkit* to refresh myself of the important notes, commitments, and statements I have made?

- When reviewing the *Code-Breaker Toolkit*, do I ensure that any updates or revised commitments and statements regarding my situation have been included or updated appropriately?

Review Point 2: Your *DART-board Goal System* toolkit

The second and equally important piece of equipment to accompany your journey through the Code and on to your success is your *DART-board Goal System toolkit*. This, of course, was the process we went through to assess all aspects of your life. From that, you were able to decide the "Deliberate Dozen" goals that you have set for yourself to achieve over the short, medium, and long term. We then nailed down the WHY and we built up the HOW to form our Goal Systems and relevant time scales for each.

Unlocking the SUCCESS Code® is a goal-setting and achievement process. Yes, there are crucial elements that we need to build before and after the goal-setting and system-building stage, but fundamentally, this book and everything to do with it is designed to help you achieve the goals, aspirations, and dreams that you have decided are critical to you. Therefore, this toolkit is hugely significant and vital for your success and happiness. Like the *Code-Breaker Toolkit* in "Review Point 1," it needs to be accurate, reflective, of your true self, and detailed and specific in the WHY, HOW, and WHEN.

Here are the key questions to review and rate your progress against. Where necessary, make sure you take time to refine and reset any actions or systems that you feel require attention or reviewing.

- Is my *DART-board Assessment Toolkit* accurately and honestly completed and accurately reflective of how I am thinking and feeling at this point regarding each of the eight themes (Health, Career, Finances, Interests, Growth, Relationships, Friends and Environment) of my life?

- From this, am I satisfied that I have identified the most "Deliberate Dozen" goals to focus upon achieving, ensuring I have a balanced mix of goals I can achieve in the short, medium, and longer term?

- Have I transferred across to my *Code-Breaker Toolkit* an accurate summary of what my "Deliberate Dozen" goals are?

- For each of my "Deliberate Dozen" goals, have I accurately and honestly completed the goal systems that underpin their achievement with specific statements, commitments, and actions to support each goal system?

Review Point 3: *Smarter Not Harder*

Throughout this book, I have referenced countless tools or aids that can and will make a positive difference in your ability to succeed and achieve every goal you have set and more from life. I have referenced the power of a vision board several times. I discussed the incredible effects on your mind and your attitude that powerful and personal affirmations can have. I mentioned applications that you can download to allow you to be mindful every day and help you to add clarity to your purpose.

The use and benefits of daily journaling are proven. Several techniques to tackle challenges you may face and to help when procrastination is a challenge have been outlined, such as my "Purpose, Goals, On Marks, Get Set, GO!!"

The point of this is to encourage you to use these tools. They can make progress easier, not harder, and while I would never expect anybody to use everything I have suggested, I would encourage you to put aside any cynical observations or worries about what others might think. This is YOUR life, and you know where you want to go and what you want to achieve, so don't be resistant to seeking and using whatever aid is available to help you get there quicker and more successfully. Work smarter, not harder!

So, here are the two key questions to review and rate your progress against, and where necessary, to take the time to refine and reset your actions or systems.

- Being truthful to myself, do I feel I am leveraging the tools I need to be making clear and positive progress through each of the Code Blocks?

- If yes, then great! However, if I feel and believe I need a new or different way to progress on a specific challenge or obstacle, am I consistent in selecting and applying the appropriate tools or techniques to move me forward?

Review Point 4: *It's In or It's Not*

One of the most common questions you will ask yourself in taking what you have learned from the SUCCESS Code® is, "When do I get the time to do all this stuff?" You will remind yourself how busy you are already with demands and responsibilities to your partner, friends, family, and possibly child-care commitments. You will quickly recall just about everything else you have going on in your life, which invariably includes a job, career, or business to run or something else equally important. All this besides sleeping, eating, socializing, and whatever else uses up your time day in, day out! I get it; you are busy.

Now, here's a big secret. Those people who we deem successful, happy, and as fulfilled as we intend to be clearly must get way more than the twenty-four hours in a day that you and I get; otherwise, how can they possibly get stuff done and still be so successful? I think we all know that every single one of us on the planet gets the same amount of time each day to use and invest, and those whom we look up to as successful often just use their time smarter than we do and prioritize their plans, actions, and needs better than the majority. They don't feel guilty when they have a time conflict; they are clear on their purpose and what they need to get done and make their decisions accordingly. That is what you need to think about and be honest and disciplined with yourself.

If you do not specifically schedule those essential tasks to enable your goal systems and actions into your diary or routine, it's unlikely they will get done. If you choose to watch two or three hours of mindless TV each night rather than invest in your future success, then do not blame others when you can't get all you need to get done the next morning. If you cannot get up one hour earlier every day to complete your exercise goal, or to sit quietly and work on mindfulness and 5-4-3-2-1 reflections, then do not be shocked when you get frustrated about the lack of progress you are making in life.

You will have enough time to be successful and achieve all of your goals if you make the right, disciplined, and structured decisions and commit these decisions into your diary or calendar and stick to them! So, here are the three key questions to review and rate your progress against, and where necessary, to make sure you take the time to refine and reset your actions or systems.

- Is my weekly time scheduled out so that I can clearly prioritize and meet all of my required goal systems and actions as well as having time for my partner, family, friends, and so on?

- When my planned schedule slips or something urgent comes up to prevent taking action today, do I take time that evening to revisit my schedule and explore ways to try and get the action or task completed quickly?

- We all need hobbies, interests, and distractions to help us relax in our lives, but am I satisfied that I have the right balance between doing/making progress and not doing/not making progress?

Review Point 5: *"Shelf-Esteem" or Action?*

This review point is designed to get you to assess the impact of applying the knowledge and lessons of the SUCCESS Code® and turning that knowledge and understanding into action. Knowledge is not power. Doing stuff, taking action, and moving forward with the knowledge you have, that is where the power is. What has been your approach to the book and then the action required? The book on its own is merely adding to your "shelf-esteem." Taking action, day in, day out, is what builds up confidence, momentum, and positive self-esteem.

Without action, nothing can be achieved in moving your life toward the achievement of the "Deliberate Dozen" goals you have set and all the incredible senses of achievement, satisfaction, happiness, and fulfilment this brings. It's impossible. And it's not just about taking action when it is easy. Going for a run in the park on a warm summer's day is often a pleasant experience, and clearly, could well be an action that will be part of your goal system on a health goal, for example. However, when the same goal system demands that you do the same run (the same action) on a cold, wet morning in winter, will you be strong enough, purposeful, and determined enough to take action? That's where success sits. Right in that moment. Taking action or not. You are worth the investment, so don't look for excuses. Don't say that it's about not having time. Don't blame external factors. It's in you to do it, so take the action necessary.

So, here are the key questions to review and rate your progress against. Where necessary, make sure you take the time to refine and reset your actions or systems.

- Am I feeling positive and certain that I am taking the required actions stated in my goal systems and feel confident that I can maintain these for the duration that each goal system requires?

- When I am unable to complete a required action for a valid reason, do I take time to evaluate the implications, and, if necessary, find alternative ways to maintain progress toward the goal?

- When it feels like a specific action is not working for me or I cannot see the progress toward a goal that I expected, will I be mentally strong enough to persevere?

- When I do persevere and continue to see little or no progress toward a goal that I am focused upon, will I look to review my actions and explore alternative actions or systems, always ensuring that I continue to take some form of action to keep progressing?

Review Point 6: *Fears and Friends*

In Review Point 5 above, the focus of my questioning was on your desire to keep taking action when you are tired, distracted, and unable to build up that motivation to get up and move even when you know you have to. In this review point, the focus is on how you assess your ability to deal with those who will drag you down and steal your dreams as well as finding those who can help, support, and raise you up to actually increase your chance and speed of success and achievement.

Let's tackle the difficult one first. You will, I am certain, come across "doubters" when you explain what you are doing and how you are focused on achieving your "Deliberate Dozen" goals and progressing toward your purpose and passion in life. It could even be your husband, wife, or partner! Maybe close family members or best friends! Often, these doubters are your colleagues or associates from work or your social scene, but some or all of these people will suggest that, "You should lower your expectations; don't be silly aiming for such goals; you'll never get them, anyway so just be satisfied with what you have."

So, what will you do? These suggestions will frequently come from people you love, and it's not that they want you to be unhappy, it's just a reflection of how the vast majority of us think and operate. You, however, know that there is so much more to life, and you are determined to go out there and get it.

You know what you must do without my reminding you, but I will anyway. One option is to sit down and explain the SUCCESS Code® to your close friends and family, why you have decided to make this change, and that you would really value their love and support in helping you progress forward. If they love you as you know they do, this is often what they indeed will do for you. The upside of this is that you will have at least one more person on your team! If these friends, family, and associates, however, continue to point out why you will not succeed, why you are wasting your time, and why these strategies and programs will never work, you have a big decision to make. In your heart, you know what the action needs to be.

On the flip side, you can never have too many supporters, mentors, and coaches on your team, so be mindful of this. Build up a small team of mentors and coaches that you can rely upon, those whom you can go to for advice and guidance and helpful and supportive discussions. Join several Facebook groups that have personal development and achievement at their core. Look out for local mastermind and network groups that you can join either in person or online. Surrounding yourself with the right people and reducing time spent with the wrong people is a key component to your future success and the speed at which you achieve it.

So, here are the key questions to review and rate your progress against. Where necessary, make sure you take the time to refine and improve your actions or systems.

- Today, at this moment, do I clearly have people in my life who are openly negative and destructive to my plans for success and achievement? If so, have I taken or decided to take clear steps to reduce or minimize these people in my life to protect my path to my goals and dreams for my life?

- Today, at this moment, have I clearly identified people or networks that can be a positive and supporting force for my plans for success and achievement? If not, then I need to. If so, then have I reached out for their support, assistance, or membership to positively improve the path to my goals and dreams for my life?

Review Point 7: *Keep Tuning the Engine*

If you have gone through the previous six SUCCESS Code® review points and rated yourself as at least eight out of ten in each or better, then this final one should be easy to score well in! I have called this "Tuning the Engine," and that is exactly what I am asking you to assess and review here. On a day-by-day basis, maybe week by week on certain disciplines or activities, are you keeping the engine tuned and working in peak condition?

You know from Code Block 6 that this is about those ten minutes at the start of every day to get your mind and attitude spot on and set up for success, when you seek time to be mindful and truly step back and remind yourself of your life's purpose, passions, and why you deserve to be happier, more successful, and fulfilled. This is about those final few moments before sleep when you program your mind to be grateful for today and ready to be successful tomorrow. It is about that discipline each day to make some reflections in your journal of what went well today and what learnings you have received to help you improve or perform even better tomorrow.

The aim here with these techniques and processes is to form *habits*, *positive habits* that will become as natural as brushing your teeth or putting a seatbelt on in the car. When you have positive, daily routines as habitual as that, purposefully done to fuel your mind and attitude with gratitude, clarity, and a reminder of what and why you are doing such an activity, you certainly do have the engine tuned and running like clockwork.

I, therefore, have only one key question for you to review and to rate your progress against, and where necessary, to make sure you take the time to refine and improve your actions or systems.

- Am I confident and satisfied that my daily schedule, from the moment of waking to the moment of sleeping, is structured well enough to provide me with daily tools, disciplines, and processes to ensure I remain clear on my purpose and actions for that day?

So, there you go. Seven reflective SUCCESS Code® Review Points that I would ask you to consider honestly and where necessary to take the required actions to get you, your mind, your goal systems, and your various toolkits to the place where they need to be to enable your success.

Whatever your find your answers or feelings were as you went through each review point, should determine which of the specific Code Blocks you may wish to revisit. The SUCCESS Code® is a cyclical process. It is designed to help you maintain and grow in your understanding, awareness and ability to keep on succeeding, achieving, growing and winning!

Compelling Action 7

Update your *Code-Breaker Toolkit* sheet under Code Block 7. Consider each of the above review points and if you feel that you are "scoring yourself" less than maybe 7 or 8 out of ten in terms of effectively applying the strategy or toolkit etc, then you should look to revisit the appropriate part of the SUCCESS Code® and increase your effectiveness and discipline as required. You have made wonderful progress in reaching this point so keep working your way through the process, and you will continue to build strength, confidence and understanding on what and how to achieve your purpose, goals and success in life and work!

Closing Thoughts

"Make your life a dazzling masterpiece. Have no limitations in your mind of what you can have in life, be in life or do in life. You possess everything you need, it's just a matter of action!"

– Steve McNicholas

My sincerest wish in writing this book was that each and every person who reads it finds at least one thing to spark them off on a journey to fulfil their dreams, live their purpose, and pursue and achieve their goals in their personal lives and in their business and professional lives. My own purpose today remains as it has been for a long time, "To inform, inspire, and help maximize the potential for all, unlocking the SUCCESS Code® to help develop winners in life and business."

I hope, therefore, that maybe just one tip, technique, idea, or maybe even a quote or a poem within the book has triggered something in you to go beyond the ordinary, to seek and build a life that you can describe as being an extraordinary life.

The book, the SUCCESS Code®, and the many code-bytes within as well as the toolkits and resources I have referenced are simply the tools. You will be the person who chooses to use them or not. I know the incredible life you can have if you decide to do just that. There are really no accidents in this universe; you were always meant to get to this point right here in your life and live the life you are today. However, there is something in you that wants much more. You have always had that feeling or sense within you; it's perhaps just been buried deep.

Well now you have another choice and it's pretty simple: You can choose ordinary and continue to live the life you do today, and all aspects of that life will likely remain as they are today. Or, you can choose extraordinary.

You can commit to building and living a life, career, or business on your terms, and based on your goals, dreams, and aspirations, and there is a way to do that.

Understand and then unlock the SUCCESS Code® for you.

Keep winning!

Steve McNicholas

About the Author

After a successful 30-year executive career across several businesses and industries, Steve McNicholas formed his own consultancy and training business, Moldan Consulting. His first book, *Recipe for Success*, co-authored with *New York Times* best-selling author Jack Canfield, reached best-seller status on Amazon in 2019.

Steve is a sought-after keynote speaker, training facilitator and personal coach who offers group programmes, seminars and workshops, all designed to help attendees to unlock the *SUCCESS Code*® and take their businesses, performance and career to the next level.

Steve has held several director and executive roles throughout his career, including positions at Santander Group, Royal Bank of Scotland and TransUnion, and consulted for several organisations in the UK. He has continuously sought to develop his business education by attending programmes at The Liverpool University Management School and at Harvard Business School.

Steve's personal focus is "to inform, inspire and maximise the potential in all – unlocking the SUCCESS Code® *to develop winners in life and business.*"

Please visit www.stevemcnicholas.com if you'd like to learn more about this book and Steve's speaking, workshops and training services.